OVER & OVER

A CATALOG OF HAND-DRAWN PATTERNS

MICHAEL PERRY
PRINCETON ARCHITECTURAL PRESS,
NEW YORK

Published by
Princeton Architectural Press
37 East Seventh Street
New York, New York 10003

For a free catalog of books, call 1.800.722.6657.
Visit our website at www.papress.com.

Edited by Nicola Bednarek
Designed by Michael Perry

Special thanks to: Nettie Aljian, Sara Bader, Dorothy Ball, Janet Behning, Becca Casbon, Penny (Yuen Pik) Chu, Russell Fernandez, Pete Fitzpatrick, Wendy Fuller, Jan Haux, Clare Jacobson, Aileen Kwun, Nancy Eklund Later, Linda Lee, Laurie Manfra, Katharine Myers, Lauren Nelson Packard, Jennifer Thompson, Arnoud Verhaeghe, Paul Wagner, Joseph Weston, and Deb Wood of Princeton Architectural Press —Kevin C. Lippert, publisher

The text in this book was set with Locator, designed by Process Type Foundry; American Typewriter; and Adobe Garamond.

Library of Congress Cataloging-in-Publication Data
Perry, Michael, 1981 July 19–
 Over and over : a catalog of hand-drawn patterns / by Michael Perry.
   p. cm.
 ISBN 978-1-56898-757-6 (alk. paper)
1. Drawing—Themes, motives. 2. Commercial art—Themes, motives. 3.
Pattern books. I. Title.
 NC754.P47 2008
 741.6—dc22
                                                                                2008002016

A CATALOG OF HAND-DRAWN PATTERNS

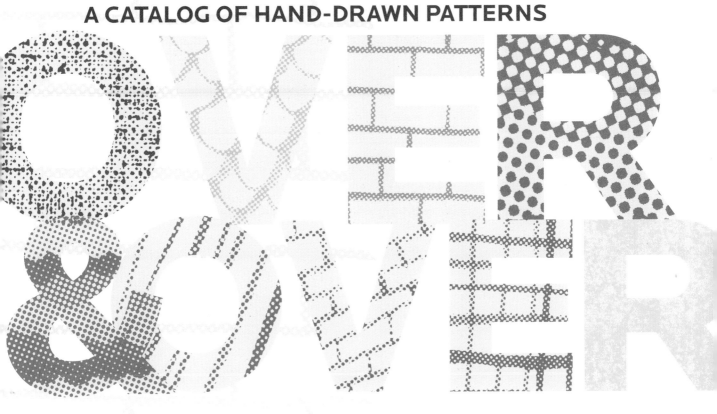

OVER & OVER

DEDICATED TO MY BROTHER CHRISTOPHER PERRY, WHOM I FORGOT TO PUT IN THE DEDICATION OF MY FIRST BOOK. I WOULD TRULY BE NOWHERE WITHOUT YOU! YOU ARE NEVER FORGOTTEN!

TABLE OF CONTENTS

PREFACE

BY MIKE PERRY

After my previous book, *Hand Job: A Catalog of Type,* was published, I knew that the celebration of things done by hand was not over for me. I wanted to explore another area of design that has interested me for a long time. My interest in patterns came about by accident. While digging through books about type, pattern books made their way into my piles and then onto my shelves, where they sat for years. Then, while working on a project, I made a quick decision to use some of these patterns. That project quickly locked into place, and I had fallen in love. The more I made patterns, the more it felt right. They started to live—as color, texture, backgrounds, foregrounds—on their own.

Patterns have been used in design forever. But in our world, where patterns surround us on everything from wallpaper to fabric, the people I was most interested in were the makers who choose to craft patterns by hand. Drawing a pattern is not the easiest way of doing it, but, when the time is spent, something magical happens. As with any drawing, you can see the maker. Each and every piece in this book is special; its pages are filled with people who are constantly pushing the boundaries and questioning what a pattern is. Some of the examples I included are made with traditional pattern usage in mind. Deanne Cheuk's patterns adorn current fashion, which is the result of collaboration. Other patterns are used in less traditional applications. Robin Cameron creates patterns to explore her interest in art, while Garrett Morin's patterns arose from an exercise for a character he has created named Eloie.

Making this book has been amazing. As each submission rolled in, I started to fantasize about using the patterns enclosed within my own work. What if I could use the camouflage made by Dan Funderburgh in a drawing that I was working on? What if I could use one of the floral patterns made by Brie Harrison as the base of a T-shirt design? And that's what patterns are meant for. Sometimes they are the end result and sometimes they are just the beginning. I hope you find the magic within each and every page of this book and spend some time examining the attention to detail that these amazing artists have devoted to their patterns.

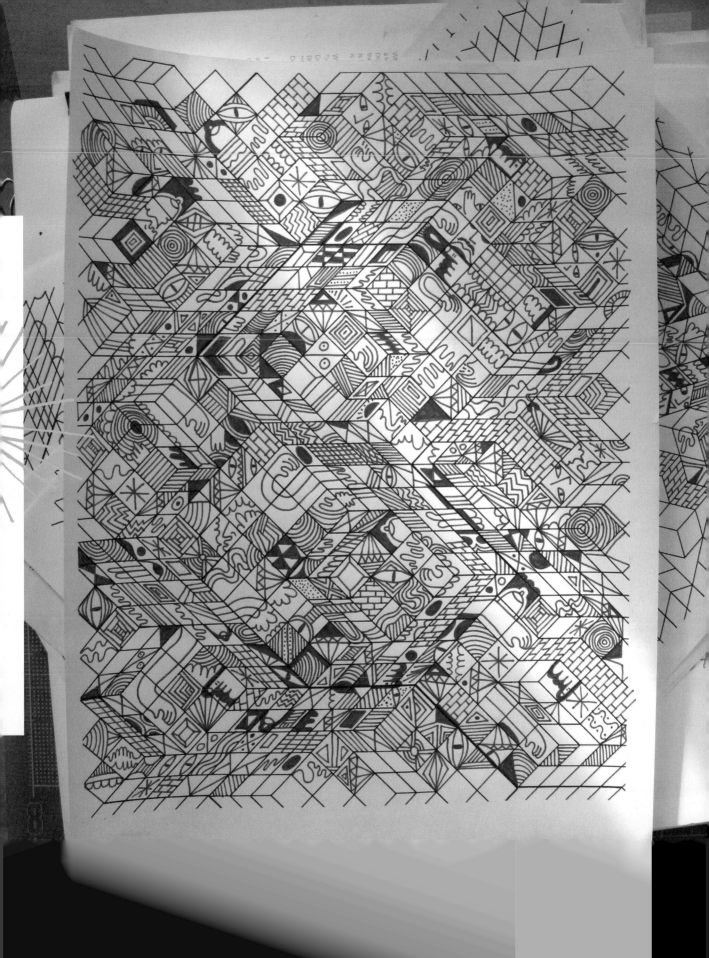

BY JIM DATZ

It was all over before we knew it.
While crate-digging in the dusty back room of a mom-and-pop stationery store, an anonymous design-hungry *otaku* uncovered a thin box of pristine Zip-A-Tone transfer sheets—an exuberant time capsule of 1980s pattern.

A Brazilian kid on eBay, while hunting for the most elusive Nike Air Force One prototypes or an obscure Geoff McFetridge rarity, impulsively clicks on a seller's "additional items," discovers a pair of Vans SK8 Highs with an Alexander Girard trefoil fabric pattern—and a vast new world of mid-century textile design in the process.

A young Scandinavian illustrator, midway through her residency at a Vancouver artists' retreat, wanders through town on a lazy Saturday of thrift stores, soy mochas, and photography—returning with a satchel full of 1970s Vera scarves, totem pole Polaroids, and driftwood sculptures to fuel her Marimekko-meets-forest-monsters print series.

A bored-to-tears East London scene kid scavenges a Deadstock cut-and-sew hoody, with allover monochrome print, and wears it (over a striped French sailor tee) to his disastrous-yet-epic inaugural gig at the Old Blue Last. The sound is utter shite, but, good goddamn, if they don't look amazing. His accidental ownership of a new effortless hybrid style/style-by-necessity spawns a technicolor-jean pointy-brogue revolution that is:

—splattered that same night across no fewer than three snapshot debauchery websites;
—almost immediately replicated the following week at any number of parties in Berlin, Paris, Tokyo, New York, and Kansas City;
—soon to hurtle toward the mainstream on wheels greased by a few only-half-serious stylists, band members, indie zine

editors, and the stroboscopic polychrome psychedelia of a labeled-and-prepackaged style/genre called "Nu Rave";
—peacocked shortly thereafter by MTV-fetishizing chroma-philes who spin off a Hypercolor hip-hop splinter group that hustles and flows in animal prints, Day-Glo gradients, silver foil Victorian engravings, and the fading fireworks of a once-emerging trend gone red giant.

Sense a pattern here?
There's something happening right now—something to do with pattern and the present, and it spans the full spectrum of fine and applied arts, from lowbrow to high style. It's a moment of cultural condensation, and what was once merely a useful motif/tactic has now become a significant movement. Even a cursory glance at fashion over the past four seasons will make it obvious that the stripe alone has subdivided into a multitude of new species worthy of a biologist's careful taxonomy.

Like most spikes in the evolution of visual culture, this one has the precise combination of timing, relevance, a latent distribution network, and ease of replication to tip it into something altogether more vital—a platform for free association and spontaneous expression. And pattern is the vehicle.

1-2-3 Repeater
It's pretty difficult to talk about visual trends without first understanding their life cycle. Trends no longer propagate in the old, linear way: incubating, gathering complexity, building momentum, and then exploding into the mainstream robust and fully formed. Technology has provided an affordable means to be on display, and overnight ubiquity is the order of the day. Small fires begin in distributed

locations across the planet, from obscure backwaters to major urban centers, and almost at the moment they begin, they are lifted, collated, named, and marketed in a willful act of pattern recognition by today's cultural curators. These days, staying small has become a legitimate challenge.

As designers, we have the privilege of seeing both sides of the process of creation and consumption. Some of us also view design as a language, an ongoing conversation between makers, both skilled and unskilled, across great distances and disciplines—evolving in real time, with every piece of new work that is pushed into the public sphere. With everything on display all of the time, most of us have abandoned the romantic notion of "originality," and have embraced a more organic process. Our work is recursive. We act as culture sponges. We manipulate flows. We consume, digest, percolate, blend, filter, make, tweak, and re-present our own work (with a vapor trail of precedents for those who know how to read them).

Each new generation has at its disposal the whole of design history (among other things). There's simply more of it, and it's increasingly accessible and visible. We can sample across decades, styles, and themes more easily every day, acting purely on a superficial affinity for those elements of the past that inspire us in our particular sliver of the present.

The only downside of this process is an increase in recombinant minutiae, as sampling culture heads toward a kind of motif-singularity, beyond which there are no smaller metagenres into which to divide. But history has proven that what we imagine is never where we ultimately arrive, and even the bleakest dystopian visions usually soften with time. Images stick around. The forgotten ones will be dusted off and paraded anew, to be used in completely original ways by our successors. The reemergence of pattern in contemporary design owes much to this process.

Japan + Anecdote

On my first trip to Asia, following the obligatory weeklong head-explosion that most visual-culture junkies experience shortly after air-dropping into Tokyo, I followed a friend's recommendation and fled for the less-populated west coast in search of a small fishing village known for its picturesque vernacular houses. While taking a brief lunch detour at a rail stop halfway, I chanced upon a rice paddy— the first opportunity I had to examine one at close range.

Rice is cultivated in terraced fields that are flooded with shallow water, beneath which are planted uniform rows of plants—a man-made grid of green sprouts that dot the surface, producing the usual parallax eye tricks when scanned at automobile speed. This pattern was immediate and obvious, but after looking closely at the entire system, another rhythm emerged: Recorded in the silt floor of the paddy were a series of snaking dashed lines—the meandering footprints left by farmers while maintaining their crop. These

spontaneous marks stood as an aesthetic counterpoint to the rational grid that resulted from the collective knowledge of generations.

Pattern can be derived from many sources. Traditional methods and extemporaneous impulse can combine to form interesting hybrids. You'll see a lot of that in the pages ahead. Just remember to look closely.

Comfort in Repetition

We are pattern-searching animals. We draw energy from activated fields, from live surfaces, from rhythm in repeat. Pattern is as much to be found as it is to be made, simultaneously organizing space and complicating it—order and disorder cohabiting.

Working with pattern can induce a meditative state. (How many of us have emerged from a stupor after a few hours of drilling into a complicated repeat, eyes glazed and head spinning with the permutations of folded space, trying to manage four overlapping borders at once, without having it look "obvious?") Occupying the conscious mind with gestural repetition permits the subconscious to do its work, and many breakthrough creative moments have risen from this sort of deliberate task making. Fortunately, our tools have also evolved to more easily enable the use of pattern in our visual repertoire.

The dot. The line. The grid. The mesh. The halftone as object. Lithographic artifacts become decorative elements. Brocades are subverted. The fill becomes the filigree.

Sum of Its Parts

Complex as it may appear, most pattern is not hermetic. All the parts are on display, easily deconstructed—a recognizable system, even to the unschooled. Perhaps this low cost of entry/high visual payoff is one of the reasons for pattern's resurgence in the popular sphere.

Or maybe we're unconsciously moving toward com—plexity in response to a decade of restraint, when a strain of austere Swiss modernism rose up to dominate the design world. The supremely rational flatness of the Helvetica evangelists, the oppressive repetition of the fashion advertising logo-and-photo crew, and the simplified vector silhouettes of a few years ago have motivated a particular group of image-makers to manifest not a trend, but a tendency—a tendency to allow pattern to animate their work with color and exuberance.

All Ahead Full

It's important to hit pause now and then, if only for the fact that it allows us to trawl the wreckage, to figure out what the hell's been going on, and to consider where it may all be headed. It is an opportunity to acknowledge the sustained force and voluminous residue of our great distributed act of improvised collaboration—an outpouring of expression that motivates each of us through inspiration, competition, and the simple compulsion to make.

If you're on the glass-half-empty team, then maybe pattern is a dying star, glimpsed on the following pages just as it goes supernova and dissipates into the dusty ether of design history, its energy distributed and dormant, awaiting a future generation to lift it up again. But if you view design (as I do) as a form of communication—a language in its own right—you've probably begun to realize that this pattern thing is not just some fleeting new slang that the kids have copped to; it is a full-blown paradigm shift in the way we speak to one another, and the ripple effect has only just begun.

EMILY C. M. ANDERSON

www.ecmanderson.net

Emily C. M. Anderson studied graphic design at the Minneapolis College of Art and Design and at the Academie voor beeldende kunst en vormgeving Arnhem, in the Netherlands. After graduation she worked as a senior designer at *Dwell* magazine in San Francisco. In 2007 she moved to New York where she has worked with MGMT design and Project Projects on jobs for the International Center of Photography, Rizzoli, *New York* magazine, Yale University, and the Design Trust for Public Space, among others. She joined the American Craft Council in August of 2007, working most recently on the relaunch of *American Craft* magazine.

opposite:
Untitled (love), 2003
Endpaper pattern for a book proposal
Hand-drawn ornaments; arranged/
repeated digitally

top left:
Untitled (green 01), 2007
Management design for
Greg Yang Design
Scanned greenery, arranged/
repeated digitally

top right:
Untitled (accessories), 2004
Background pattern sketches for poster
Scanned tulle, necklaces, beads;
arranged/repeated digitally

BEATA BOUCHT

www.beataboucht.com

Beata Boucht received her MFA in graphic design and illustration from Konstfack, University College of Arts, Crafts, and Design in Stockholm, Sweden, in the spring of 2007. She works mainly in various fields of illustration, creating drawings for magazines, animated music videos, advertisements, and books, but also produces graphic identities and logotypes. Her ambition is to create a wide range within her company, combining commercial projects with exhibitions and workshops. She sees illustration as something exploratory—"to illustrate something" in the sense of bringing out and rendering visible. She enjoys working on very different projects where she can challenge herself and find a balance between the methodical and the intuitive. Working part-time as art director for the feminist culture magazine *Bang* in Sweden, she tries to use her work to persuade others to embrace her views. She uses patterns in almost all of her illustrations in one way or another, often by building piles and islands of them. Her aim is to focus even more on them in the future since they are so meditative and make her happy.

this spread:
Flora for Lisa, 2007
School project
Pencil

22–25:
Diamond Cut Diamond, 2006
School project
Pencil

MANIFESTO
DIAMOND
CUT
DIAMOND

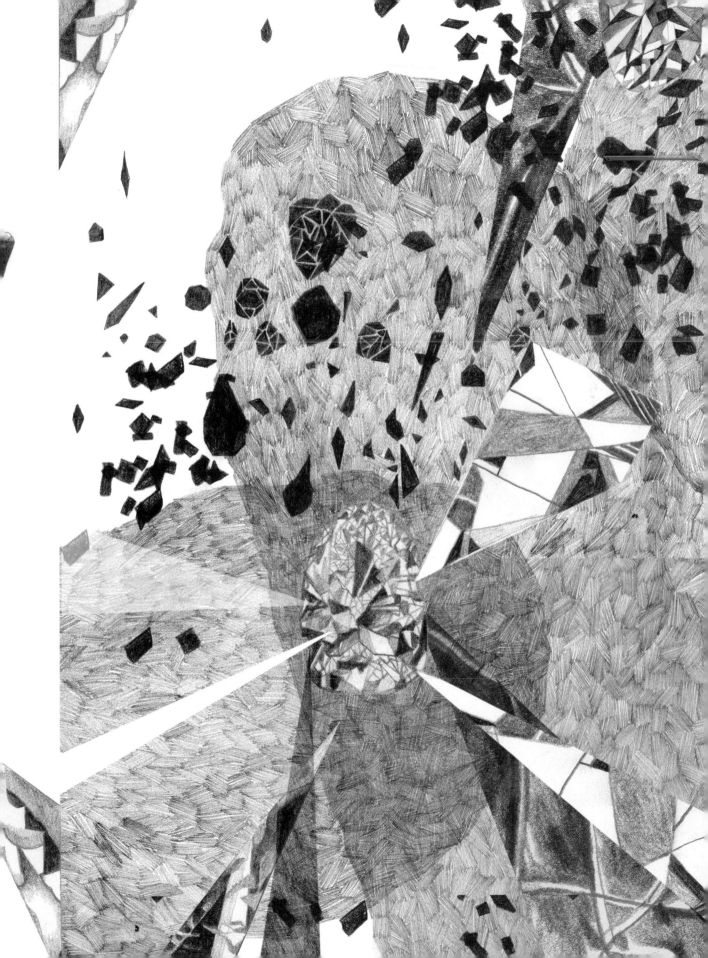

NOAH BUTKUS

www.noahbutkus.com

Growing up in the woods of Connecticut, Butkus found himself spending all of his time with skateboards and comic books. This is where he found most of his inspiration, and, for the most part, still does. His first widely recognized work appeared on graphics for Burton Snowboards. This was followed by commissions for posters, ads, catalogs, and product design from a wide variety of companies and concerns.

opposite:
Untitled, 2006
Ladies & Gentlemen magazine
Pen

top:
Various Drawings, 2006–07
Personal project
Pen

28–29:
Wallpaper, 2006
Burton Snowboards Japan Office
Pen

30:
Secret Hangout, compilation, 2007
Money Studies
Pen

31:
Wallpaper, 2006
Burton Snowboards Japan Office
Pen

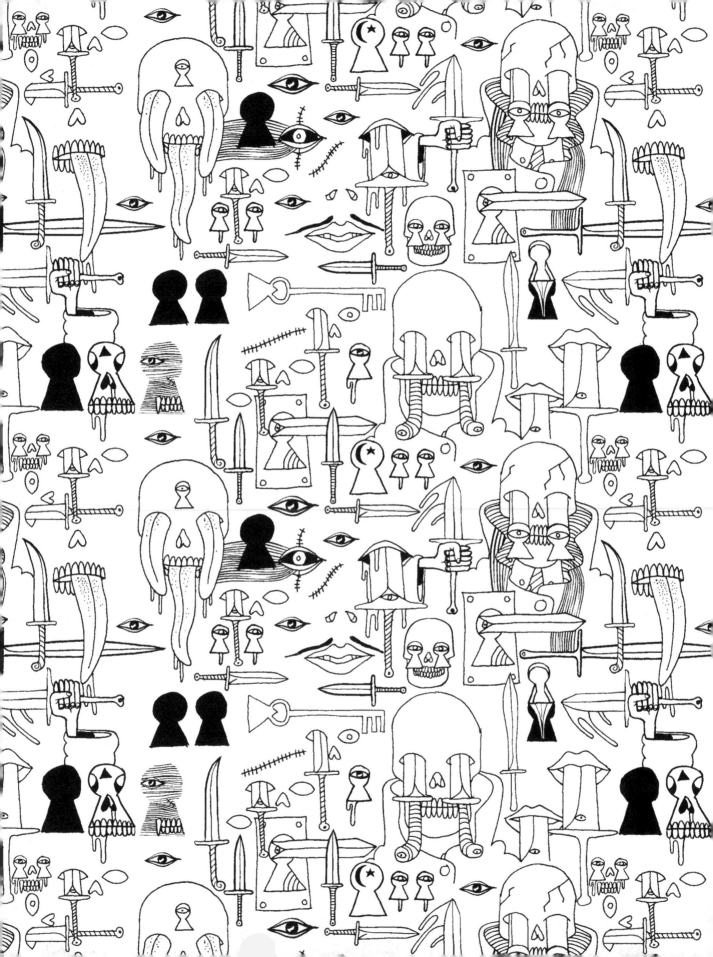

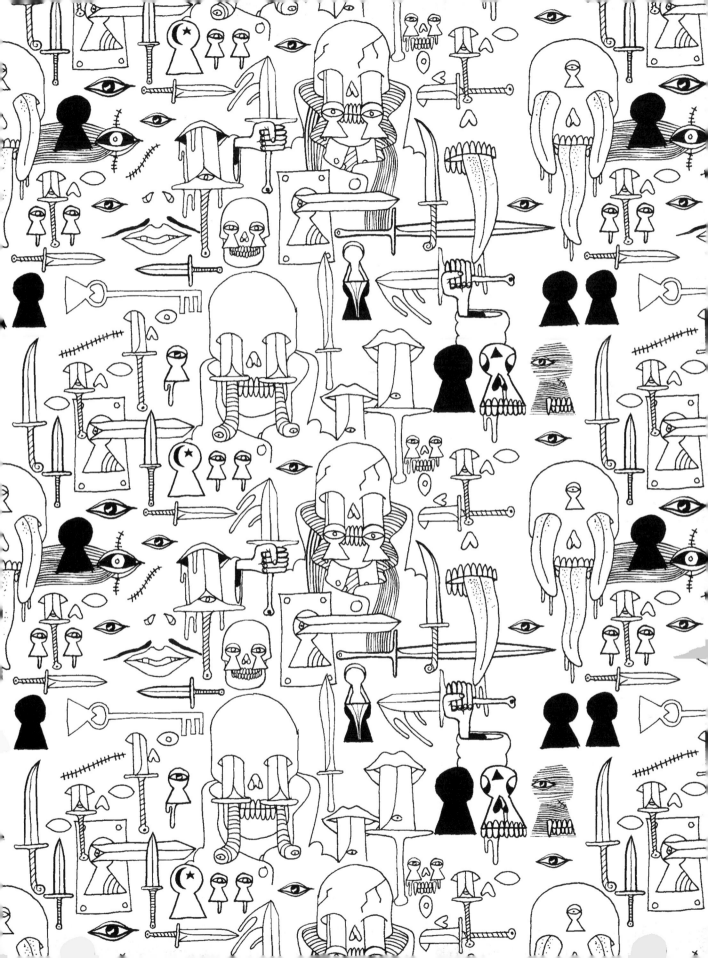

THE
BLOWN
MIND

ROBIN CAMERON

www.rocamm.com

Robin Cameron graduated with a BA in design from Emily Carr Institute of Art and Design, Vancouver, in 2004. Based in New York City, she has shown work in Vancouver, Toronto, Seattle, Chicago, and Tokyo. Her focus lies in drawing with an affinity for the hand-touched and typography. Her illustrations and designs have been published in *Arkitip*, *Adbusters* magazine, *Made* magazine, *GOOD* magazine, the *Walrus*, and the *New York Times*.

opposite:
The Blown Mind, 2006
Personal project
Ink and gouache

top:
Collage Blobs, 2006
Personal project
Collage

34:
Encourage Opinions, 2007
Personal project
Ink drawing

35:
Faith, 2006
Personal project
Ink drawing

36–37:
The Study of Light in the Blob Galaxy, 2007
Personal project
Ink and gouache drawing

DEANNE CHEUK

www.deannecheuk.com

Deanne Cheuk is an art director, illustrator, and artist from Perth, Western Australia, the most isolated city in the world. She got her first job as a magazine art director at the age of nineteen, the same year she graduated from university with a degree in graphic design. Since then, Cheuk has art directed or designed many magazines, including, most recently, *Tokion* magazine.

Cheuk's art direction is heavily influenced by her illustrative work and she is renowned for her illustrative typography. She has been commissioned by such companies as Nike, Converse, Sprint, ESPN, and MTV2 and is a contributor to *Vogue Nippon*, *Dazed & Confused*, *The FADER*, *Black-Book*, *Flaunt*, the *Guardian*, and the *New York Times Magazine*. She has worked with David Carson, Doug Aitken, and Conan O'Brien. In 2006, Target launched a line of products designed by Cheuk, and the year 2005 saw the release of her first book, *Mushroom Girls Virus*, which sold out world-wide in three months. Cheuk also self-publishes a nonprofit contributor-based graphic zine called *Neomu*. She lives in New York City.

opposite:
Coco Confetti, 2006
Sue Stemp, fall/winter 2006
Textile pattern

top:
Hand Print, 2006
Liness
Fabric print

40–41:
Holiday Paper, 2006
American Institute for Graphic Arts (AIGA)
Wrapping paper

42–43:
Paris Pyramids, 2006
Deanne Cheuk brand for
Threegee Co, Japan
Textile design

44–45:
Who Can It Be Now, 2006
Deanne Cheuk brand for
Threegee Co, Japan
Textile design

44

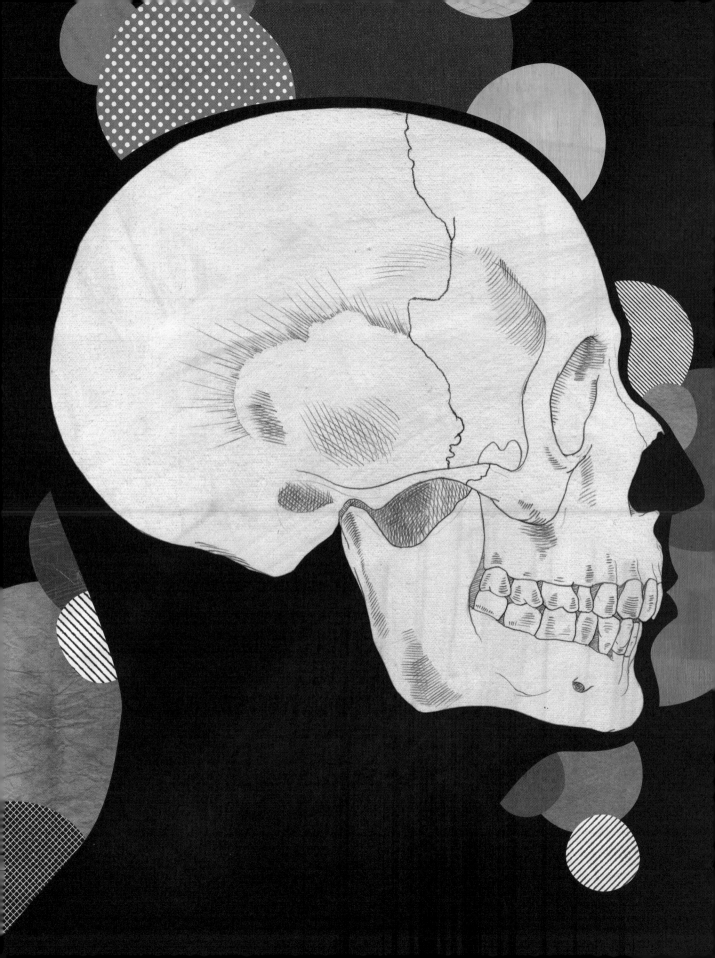

MARCO CIBOLA

www.novestudio.com

Marco Cibola is a freelance illustrator and graphic designer working out of Dundas, Ontario. Cibalo has been recognized in national and international publications such as *American Illustration* (online), *Applied Arts, Arkitip, Color Magazine, The Drama, Empty,* and *Juxtapoz.* Selected clients include ESPN, the *Financial Times,* the *New York Times, Nylon, Reader's Digest, SWINDLE* magazine, *Time* magazine, and the *Walrus.*

opposite:
Untitled, 2006
Personal project
Mixed media

top:
Untitled, 2006
Time magazine
Collage

48:
Untitled, 2006
Time magazine
Collage

49:
Untitled, 2005
Personal project
Collage

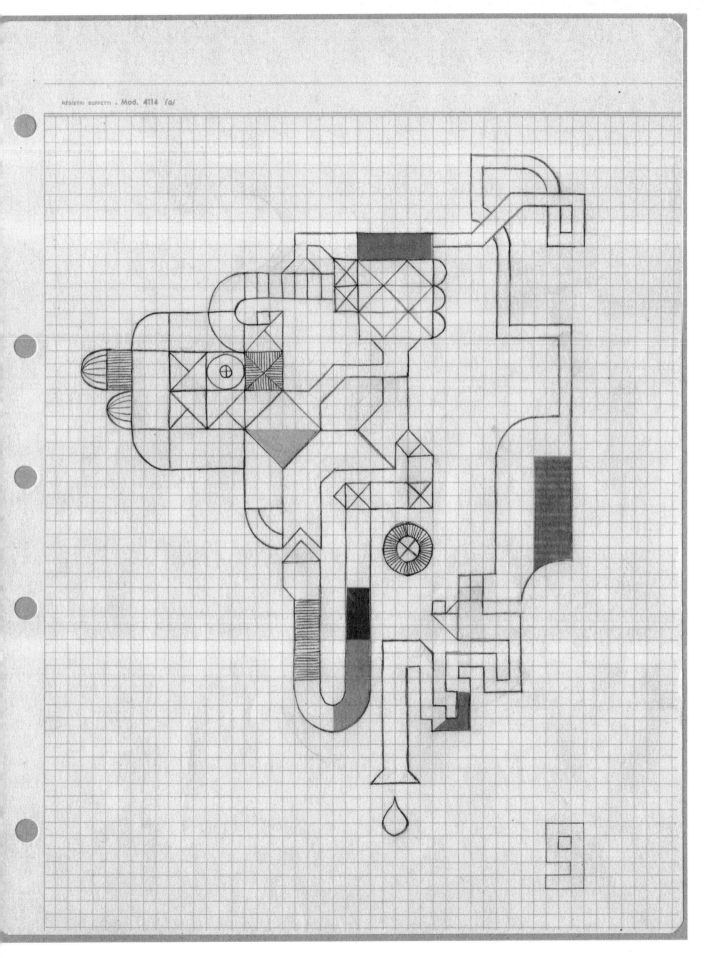

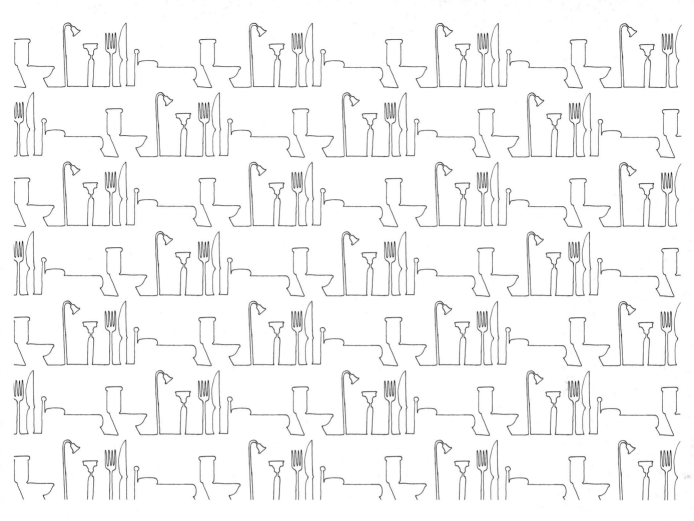

BRYAN COLLINS

www.bryan-collins.com

Bryan Collins has an unconventional background as an art director. His first graphic design job came when he befriended a film editor, who trained him in the basics of motion graphics and editing. During the peak of the dot-com era, he fell in love with interactive media and gained experience at several Internet advertising firms. Redirected by layoffs, he started working intensely as a free agent—designing flyers, logos, websites, animations, and CD packaging.

In 2001 he moved to New York City and began freelance work for firms such as GHava, Honest, EGO, and Wolff Olins. Collins currently works for a popular American clothing retailer that your little brother or sister is wearing at this very moment.

opposite:
Organic, 2007
Personal project
Pen

top:
Life Line, 2007
Personal project
Pen

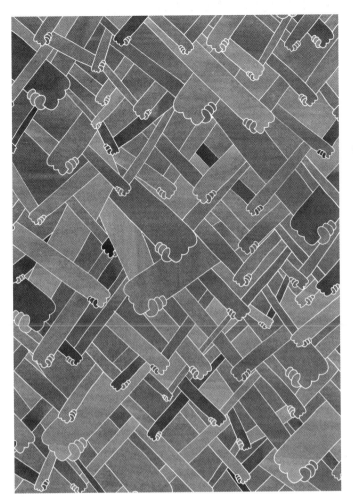

DAMIEN CORRELL

www.damiencorrell.com

Originally from Philadelphia, Damien Correll is a twenty-five-year-old freelance designer, maker, and illustrator living and working in Brooklyn, New York, where he shares a studio space at Rad Mountain. Since graduating from the University of the Arts in 2004, he has worked on a number of projects for Urban Outfitters, Nike, Zoo York, and Polyvinyl Record Co. and has been featured in the pages of *New York* magazine, *IdN*, the *New York Times Magazine*, and *Faesthetic*. He uses pattern whenever he can.

opposite:
Untitled Print, 2007
Private commission
Marker

top left:
Hand Holding, 2006
Faesthetic magazine
Watercolor and pen

top right:
Nice to Be Nice, 2007
Personal project
Custom type and patterns

54–55:
Number One Fan Club, 2006
Personal project
Newsprint zine

56–57:
Shhh, 2007
Spread in artist zine *Something Secret*
Marker and pattern collage

JIM DATZ

www.neitherfishnorfowl.com

Jim Datz is a multidisciplinary designer and illustrator who recently moved to London, following four years as art director of the Urban Outfitters web and catalog division. Raised on the beaches of southern New Jersey and a steady diet of skating, surfing, listening to punk rock, and taunting nonlocals, he eventually decamped to Philadelphia to study architecture at the University of Pennsylvania. During a summer in Japan, he was bitten hard by the fast-forward-culture bug and returned home with a head full of ideas, abandoning a promising career to play in the fields of the superficial and trendy. It was a really, really good decision.

opposite:
Octopop, 2007
Personal project
Digitally manipulated ink drawing, textures

top left:
Harlequin Disaster, 2007
Personal project
Digitally manipulated ink drawing,
sampled type, and textures

top right:
Heart City, 2007
Anonymous client
Digitally manipulated ink drawing

60–61:
My Home Is..., 2007
Spread from *WishWell* magazine
Digitally manipulated ink drawing,
sampled textures

KEETRA DEAN DIXON

www.fromkeetra.com

Keetra Dean Dixon is an art director, designer, and experiential strategist working under the handle FromKeetra. Her often-frazzled workshop pushes its focus toward noncommissioned work, but occasionally finds the lure of a shiny client job too seductive to resist. FromKeetra straddles a wide set of mediums in the pursuit of 2D, 3D, installation-, and event-based projects. Dixon developed many of her group's founding aspirations during her master's studies at the Cranbrook Academy of Art. A vow to follow her evolving obsessions keeps the studio running endlessly on new paths in the pursuit of wonder, delight, and irreverent whimsy. Dixon's work has been featured in a number of exhibits and publications, most recently including *Type Addicted* by Victionary, *The Royal* magazine, and *Tactile: High Touch Visuals* by Die Gestalten.

opposite:
Flower Star, 2007
Personal project
Acrylic on paper

top left:
Bow, 2007
Personal project
Acrylic and pencil on paper

top right:
Fans, 2007
Personal project
Acrylic on paper

RAY FENWICK

www.coandco.ca/ray

Ray Fenwick is an artist, illustrator, and typographic thing-maker living in Halifax, Nova Scotia, Canada. A former improv comedian and theater school dropout, Fenwick now occupies himself making drawings, comics, and patterns for clients such as Blue Q, Country Music Television, If'n Books, Nickelodeon, Tiny Showcase, Urban Outfitters, and others. His award-winning comic *Hall of Best Knowledge* will be published in early 2008 by Fantagraphics.

opposite:
Nobody, 2007
Personal project
Pen and computer

top:
Disfluency Toile, 2006
Personal project
Pen and computer

66–67:
The Battle of Excelsior
Gulch, 2007
Naked & Angry
Pen and computer

68–69:
Beasts endpaper, 2007
Fantagraphics
Pen and computer

70:
Maynard and Jennica, 2007
Houghton Mifflin
Pen and computer

71:
Novelty Letters, 2006
Personal project
Pen and computer

JUSTIN FINES

www.demo-design.com

DEMO is the moniker and freelance umbrella for designer Justin Fines. Founded in Detroit in 1997, DEMO has created work for clients big and small, with projects ranging from record covers to corporate identities, T-shirts, motion design and direction, skateboards, books, and more. DEMO is headquartered at Rad Mountain at the Old American Can Factory, which is located in the Gowanus district of Brooklyn, New York.

opposite and top left:
Open Up, 2006
Personal project
Pen and computer

top right:
Zoo York Artists Series
Skateboard, 2006
Zoo York
Pen and computer

74:
Symbol or Signifier?, 2007
Threadless Select
Pen and computer

75:
Traffic, 2007
Threadless Select
Pen and computer

DAN FUNDERBURGH

www.danfunderburgh.com

Dan Funderburgh is the son of two biologists and spent several of his formative years in Kansas. He is a midfielder for the prestigious Chinatown Soccer Club located on the Lower East Side of New York City. His designs can be seen on T-shirts, skateboards, and on his line of wallpaper which can be found on the walls of stores such as Urban Outfitters as well as in the permanent collection of the Cooper-Hewitt National Design Museum.

opposite:
Flower Pedal, 2007
Personal project
Hand-screened paper

top left:
Central Park, 2007
Personal project
Hand-screened paper

top right:
Carcinogenic Wallpaper, 2005
Waiting Room magazine
Pen and computer

78–79:
Quilted Camo, 2006
SWINDLE magazine
Pen and computer

80:
Untitled, 2005
Self-promotion and
season's greetings
Pen and computer

81:
American Gothic, 2007
Personal project
Pen

82:
Hold East Skateboard, 2007
5boro NYC
Pen and computer

83:
Manhattan Storage, 2007
5boro NYC
Pen and computer

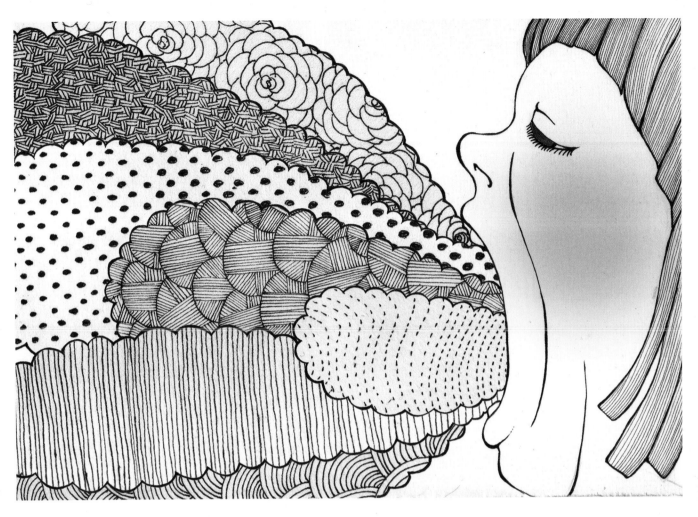

YOKO FURUSHO

www.yokofurusho.com

Yoko Furusho was born in Tokyo and studies illustration at the School of Visual Arts in New York. Some of her work was chosen for the *American Illustration* 26 web gallery.

opposite:
Snow, 2006
Personal project
Mixed media

top:
Smoke, 2007
Personal project
Mixed media

86–87:
World, 2007
Personal project
Mixed media

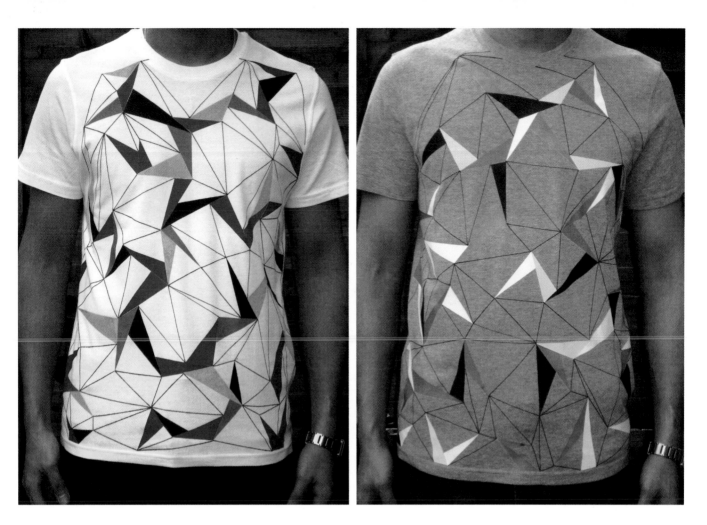

MELVIN GALAPON

www.mynameismelvin.co.uk

no-one Installation and T-Shirts, 2007
no-one boutique
Multi-colored crystallized form drawn onto
interior white walls and applied to T-shirts

Originally from the northwest of England and now living in central London, Galapon can often be found wandering the streets with his sketchbook in his back pocket and his trusty iPod shuffle to keep him company. This does not make him sound very productive, but this is where he gets a lot of his inspiration. Galapon is not a fan of keeping to one style, and his work floats between different techniques and materials. It is this inability to stick to one style that keeps him striving to find the new interesting thing for the month ahead. All that said, he has developed an interest in sticky-back vinyl, which occasionally appears in his work. Galapon's projects have appeared in *Semi-Permanent 06 Book* and *RIOT* magazine in Australia. He won the Howies Art Think 2006 competition, has exhibited work at the Magma Bookstore in London, and is studying for an MA in communication design at Central Saint Martins College of Art and Design. Recent clients include YCN, Howies, the *New York Times*, the *Guardian*, *Wallpaper**, and no-one boutique, London.

ANNA GIERTZ

www.annagiertz.se

With an MA in graphic design and illustration from Konstfack, University College of Arts, Crafts, and Design in Stockholm, Sweden, Giertz is a freelancer based in Stockholm. She has been fascinated with patterns since working on a series of wallpaper based on the novel *The Picture of Dorian Gray* by Oscar Wilde, and is inspired by popular culture, music, friends, nature and biology, magazines, and books. She has been working with illustrations and patterns for magazines, books, graphic profiles, wallpaper, prints for T-shirts, CD covers, and wall paintings, and has exhibited her work in group shows in Stockholm, Cologne, and London.

opposite:
Bleaching Agent, 2007
Personal Project
Pencil

top:
Untitled, 2006
Amelia's Magazine
Mixed media

92–93:
Untitled, 2007
Personal project
Mixed media

94–95:
Leafs, 2006
Personal project
Mixed media

96–97:
The Picture of Dorian Gray, 2004
Personal project
Pen and ink

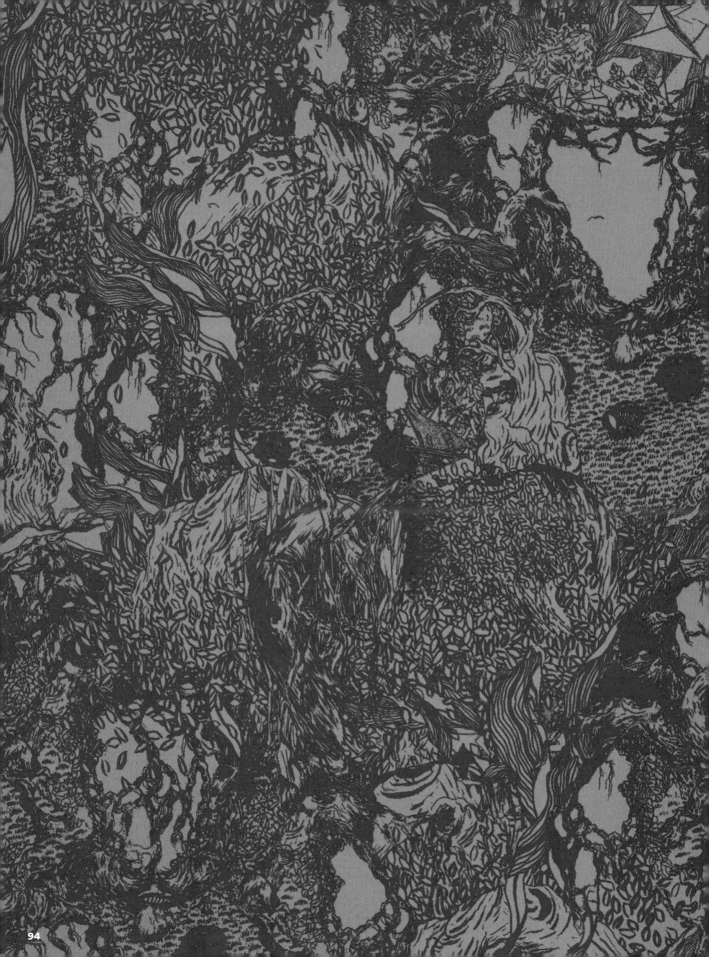

GINA AND MATT

www.ginaandmatt.com

Gina Triplett and Matt Curtius met while attending art school at the Maryland Institute College of Art in Baltimore. Now living in Philadelphia, they work together and have completed artwork for clients that include Starbucks, Target, and *Time* magazine.

opposite:
Bitter Milk, 2005
Picador
Acrylic paint

top:
Floral Pattern, 2007
Personal project
Acrylic paint, ink, and computer

GLUEKIT

www.csleboda.com

Working under the moniker of Gluekit, Christopher Sleboda and Kathleen Burns create images, illustrations, and designs. "Glue is good," says Sleboda, "it holds everything together." Their work has appeared in *Wired*, *GQ*, *Spin*, *New York* magazine, *PRINT*, and *HOW*. They recently cofounded Part of It, which works with artists to create products about causes they are passionate about. Sales from the products benefit charities chosen by the artists. Patterns permeate both their personal and commissioned work.

opposite:
Wood/Brick, 2007
Personal project
Pen

top left:
Army, 2007
Personal project
Experiment with texture

top right:
Numbers, 2007
Personal project
Pen

102:
Faces, 2007
Urban Outfitters
Pen and computer

103:
Bricks and Drips, 2007
Personal project
Pen

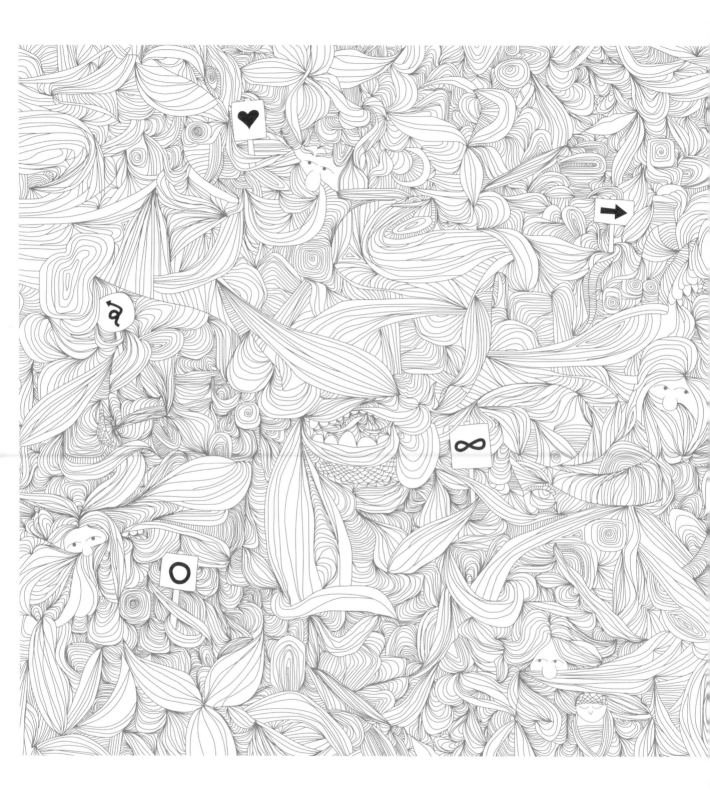

JASON GNEWIKOW

www.publicstudio.org

Jason Gnewikow is a graphic designer and occasional musician living and working in Brooklyn, New York. He spent the majority of his twenties rambling the globe, writing and playing music with the indie rock outfit The Promise Ring. In 2003 he relocated to Brooklyn from the Midwest and opened the Public Studio. He is passionate about print design, typography, printmaking, and tiny nuggets of music. His patterns appear in both his personal and professional work.

opposite:
Mustache Psych, 2005
Personal project
Silkscreen print

top left:
Optical, 2006
Personal project
Silkscreen print

top right:
Snowden, Anti-Anti *Album Cover,* 2007
Jade Tree
Offset print

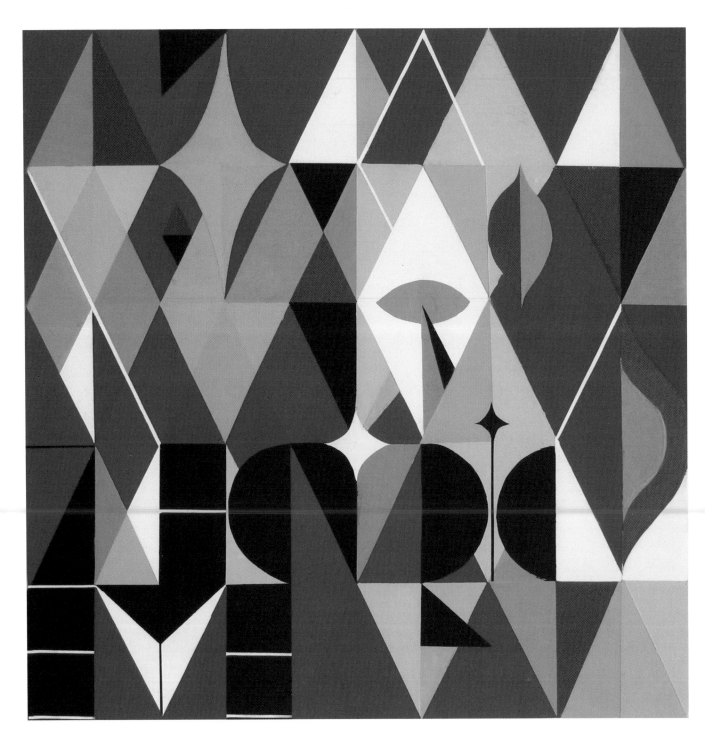

WYETH HANSEN

www.wyethhansen.com

Wyeth Hansen is a freelance designer and artist based in Brooklyn, New York, working in video, audio, and printed material. Born and raised in the armpit of California and relocated to the Northeast, Hansen's work is a blend of West Coast vibes and East Coast rigor. Raised on a creative diet of psychedelic poster art and Talking Heads albums, Hansen blends the bold and colorful transmuted typographic imagery of the psychedelic arts with the reductive and analytic minimalism of late 1970s art-funk-rock. He has exhibited work on both coasts and across the pond; clients include MTV, VH1, the AIGA, Sundance, 2K by Gingham, Ghostly International Records, a legion of design studios throughout the city, and various publications.

opposite:
Electric Eye no. 1, Life Long
Action Adventure, 2007
Riviera Gallery, Brooklyn
Gouache and silkscreen on wood

top:
Crazy Diamond/Shape of Things, 2006
2K by Gingham
Cut paper, digital collage

108–9:
Cloud of Confusion, 2007
Personal project
Ink on paper, digital collage

NAUSHA
PREDICTABILITY
SHRINKING RELEVANCE
BILLS
THE IRREVERSIBLE MARCH OF TIME
HUBRIS
IMPOTENCE
PLUS SMALL THOUGHTS
SPRING BREAK
SHADOW GOVERNMENT
WARS OF ATTRITION
PRAGMATISM
BITS
ENVY
THE PLAGUE
ADVERTISING
PSYCHOLOGY
CHAGRIN
LEISURE
DILIGENCE
UNSPOKEN RULES
FAME
LOOSE ENDS
DOUBLE MEANINGS
OBSCURE REFERENCES
CASTRATION
FEAR
IMMINENT DOOM
STARVING PEOPLE IN OTHER COUNTRIES
COMPROMISE
SHATTERED DREAMS
MISSED CONNECTIONS
AMBIVALENCE
FUCKS
DUTY
MISTAKES NESS
THE "NEW"

TREMOR ON THE LINE

HARDISTY DISK 2003
WWW.HARDISTY-DISK.COM

J. NAMDEV HARDISTY

www.m-v-a.com

J. Namdev Hardisty uses pens, pencils, paper, and computers to make drawings, T-shirts, posters, and publications. His creations are either all design or all art, but in both cases, his best work is usually a bad idea drawn out as far as it can go. Under the banner of Midwest Visual Agency (MVA), he produces solo works and collaborates with his wife, photographer Kimberlee Whaley. Recent self-published MVA projects include the *Dipset Bootleg Series*, a T-shirt line exploring the mythology of the Harlem-based rappers The Diplomats, and the *Supreme Mathematics Series*, a set of motivational posters where Swiss typography and Slim Thug finally meet. He is also a founding member of the Minneapolis artist collective/gang Labour.

opposite and top left:
Argyle, 2006
Personal project
Pen

top right:
Tremor on the Line, 2003
Hardisty-Disk Records
Pen/photocopy

112–13:
Ghost Call, 2003
Hardisty-Disk Records
Pen/photocopy

114:
Bubbles, sketch book page, 2005
Personal project
Pen

115:
Ghost Call Raw Material, 2003
Hardisty-Disk Records
Pen /photocopy

JOHN WIESE GHOST CALL

JOHN WIESE GHOST CALL

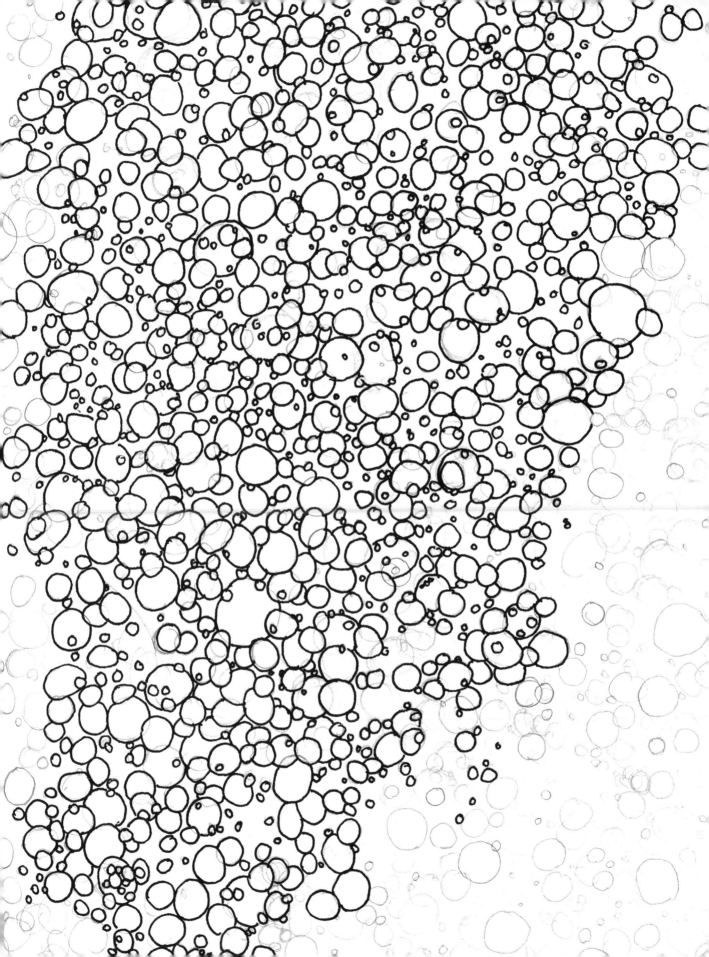

BRIE HARRISON

www.briedee.com

Brie Harrison graduated from the University of Brighton in England in 2003 with a degree in fashion textiles design. Soon after, she moved to New York City and worked for Design Works International, where she learned how to design using the computer. She then returned to England in the summer of 2004 and used this skill for Accessorize, where she designed fashion prints for bags, hats, scarves, lingerie, and beachwear. In 2007 she left to start a freelancing career, selling her artworks through the print division of Colorfield Design Studio, based in London and New York. She also works on projects for companies such as WGSN, a trend prediction website, and intends to start her own stationery line. The creation of all kinds of patterns forms a large part of her work.

opposite:
Untitled Floral, 2007
Personal project
Pen and computer

top:
Untitled Floral, 2007
Personal project
Pen and computer

118:
Untitled Floral, 2007
Personal project
Pen and computer

119:
Untitled Floral, 2007
Personal project
Pen and computer

120–21:
Untitled Floral, 2008
Personal project
Pen and computer

PUBLIC SPIRIT AND MOBS

GEORGE F. SIMMONS 1814-1855

A mob is like a wild animal broken from its lair, and is hardly more guided by any principle of reason. The contagion of blind feelings, and the very peculiar excitability of an acting multitude, and the bad passions that take that opportunity to vent themselves, and the malice which then has free play, and, hardly less, the mistaken enthusiasm which imagines something which is not there, and does the more mischief for its honesty, all swelled by idleness, and dissipation, combine to make of a multitude of men athing, under the guidance of no soul, having even no intelligent instincts, monstrous in its form, and ferocious in its purposes, a wild and awful force, before which authority and right fall and are trampled in the dust.

AUGUST HEFFNER

www.augustheffner.com

Peter August Heffner was born in an antique store in Missouri and, many years later, received a BFA in design from Kansas State University. He has since found his way to New York to work as a designer and typographer. Under such notable designers as Matteo Bologna and Stephen Doyle he has worked for clients who include Martha Stewart, Johnson & Johnson, Stephen Colbert, HarperCollins, Rizzoli Milan, Fisher-Price, *Vanity Fair*, and Nonesuch Records. As a freelance designer, he has also created work for the Guggenheim Museum, Coca-Cola, the American Red Cross, and Immortal Records. He lives in Brooklyn, works in Manhattan, and enjoys riding his bicycle betwixt the two. His use of patterns creates simple complexity.

opposite:
Public Spirit & Mobs, 2007
Public Domain
One-color offset print

top left:
Winners, 2007
Winner Collective
Pen

top right:
Black & White Rainbow, 2007
Personal project
Pen and computer

KIRK HIATT

www.kirkhiatt.net

Kirk Hiatt is an illustrator who lives and works in Philadelphia, Pennsylvania. He graduated from the Minneapolis College of Art and Design in 2006 with a degree in fine arts but lately has placed all of his focus on his illustration work. To him, the great thing about being involved with designers and illustrators is the never-ending supply of collaborations and the dialogue that is created between like-minded individuals working together.

opposite:
Pestilence (+ Detail), 2006
Personal project
Xerox transfers

top left:
Palatial Summer Home, 2007
Personal project
Marker, pen, pencil, and paint

top right:
Prism Head, 2006
Personal project
Marker, pencil, and India ink

126–27:
Bring the Noise, 2007
Personal project
Marker and pen

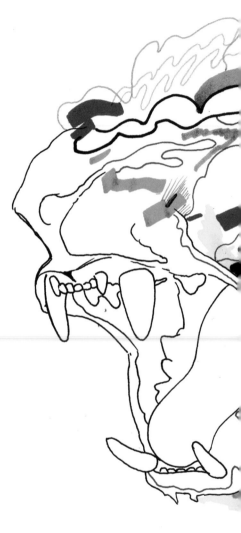

MARIO HUGO

www.loveworn.com

Mario Hugo is a New York–based artist and designer. Though he spends an inordinate amount of time in front of his computer, Hugo still feels most honest with a pencil and two or more sheets of paper. His clients include Dolce & Gabbana, Britain's Channel 4, and *W* magazine. His personal artwork has been featured in a number of publications and exhibitions worldwide.

opposite:
Nowhere Again, 2007
Personal project for Vallery exhibition
Embroidery on organic hemp/silk blend

top:
Twilight, 2007
Personal project
Digital composition

130–31:
With Great Ceremony, 2007
Personal project for Vallery exhibition
Graphite, China ink, and acrylic on torn book leafs

132–33:
And It Was Left Void, 2007
Personal project for Vallery exhibition
Graphite and acrylic on torn book leafs

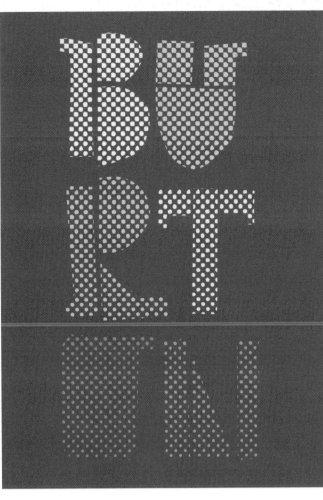

I-MANIFEST

www.i-manifeststudio.com

Matt Benson and Aaron Pollick of I-Manifest's approach involves discussion, intuition, and exploration. This allows the studio to create work that feels consistently fresh and genuine. I-Manifest's capabilities range from art direction and design to illustration and animation, for both print and interactive media. The studio's clients include Rome Snowboards, Burton Snowboards, *Dime* magazine, and Dub War NYC.

opposite:
Burton Logo, 2006
Burton Snowboards
Collaged patterns

top left:
Burtontype, 2006
Burton Snowboards
Collaged patterns

top right:
Untitled, 2006
Burton Snowboards
Collaged patterns

JEREMYVILLE

www.jeremyville.com

Jeremyville is an artist, product designer, animator, and human. He is the editor of the books *Vinyl Will Kill!* and *Jeremyville Sessions*, and initiated the "sketchel" project: satchels featuring the works of over five hundred artists, including Beck, Geneviève Gauckler, and Gary Baseman. His art was included in a group show at the concept store Colette in Paris in 2007, and has appeared in numerous design books published by such companies as Victionary, MTV, Magma Books, Laurence King, and Taschen. His work has appeared in magazines such as *Vapors, XLR8R, Wallpaper**, and *Juxtapoz*. Jeremyville's clients include Converse, Rossignol, Coca-Cola, Kidrobot, Wooster Collective, Super Rad Toys, and Corbis. He splits his time between studios in Sydney, Australia, and New York City. He collects rare T-shirts, sneakers, toys, and denim.

top right:
Voices in my Head, 2007
Lucasfilm, curated by Dov Kelemer
Custom life-size Darth Vader helmet

138:
Skull Scream, 2007
Personal project
Fabric design

139:
Jeremyville bzzzz, 2007
Personal project
Fabric design

opposite:
Untitled, 2007
Personal project
Fabric design

top left:
Mural for 55 DSL, painted live, 2006
55 DSL
Mural

140:
Jeremyville Organs, 2007
Personal project
Fabric design

141:
Acid Days, 2007
Personal project
Fabric design

140

LUNG

www.perishfactory.com

Lung is an artist from London. He likes making drawings, paintings, video art, and noise, and sometimes cakes.

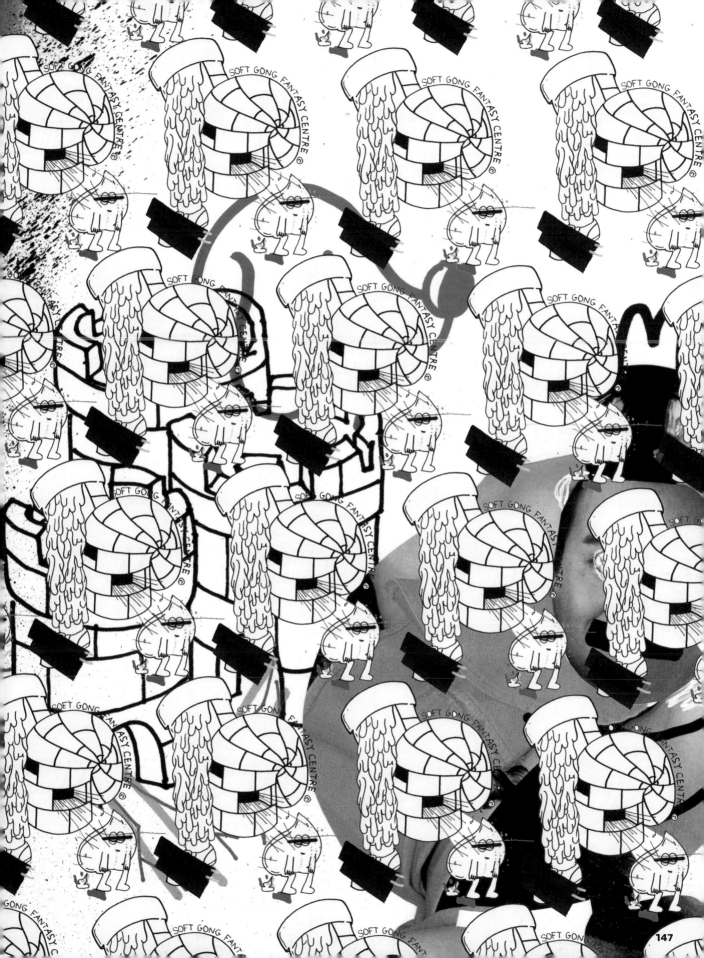

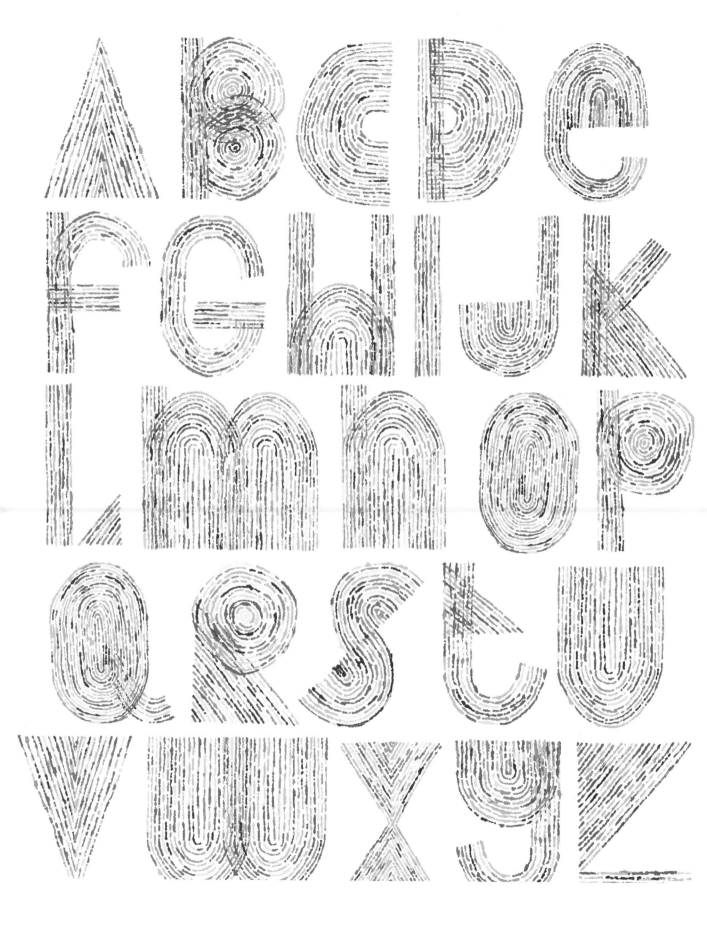

BLAKE E. MARQUIS

www.camecrashing.com

Blake E. Marquis is a designer, illustrator, and stuff maker living in Cambridge, Massachusetts. Since studying design at the Pratt Institute School of Art and Design, he has done projects for clients such as Banana Republic, GreeNYC, MySpace, the *New York Times Magazine*, and Volvo.

opposite:
Rainbow Alphabet, 2006
SWINDLE magazine
Pen

top:
Chicken Pattern, 2007
Personal project
Three-color silkscreen

152:
Untitled (diamond eye glasses), 2007
Personal project
Silkscreen on handmade paper

153:
Hasid, Brooklyn Landlord 2004, 2006–07
Came Crashing
Fabric pattern

STEFAN MARX

www.livincompany.de

Stefan Marx is an illustrator. He was born in 1979 and lives in Hamburg, Germany. The first and the last thing in his day is drawing. He tries to describe his world, his thoughts, and his views on the real world with his illustrations and paintings. Marx publishes small zines that include his works and thoughts, which derive from his love of sketchbooks and all things in books. In addition, he runs a small label called the Lousy Livincompany, where he produces T-shirt designs in small editions, so that his friends can wear them too. His patterns can be seen on a variety of forms from pajama bottoms to skatedecks.

opposite:
House Pattern, 2006
Cleptomanicx
Pen

top:
Spike Pattern, 2005
Cleptomanicx
Pen

156–57:
Hamburg Holiday, 2004
Cleptomanicx
Pen

158–59:
Fruit Pattern, 2007
Cleptomanicx
Pen

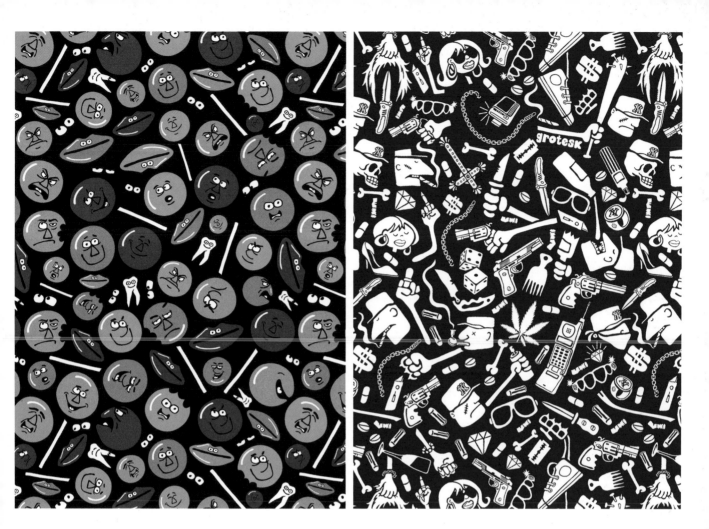

KIMOU MEYER

www.grotesk.to

Hailing from Geneva, Switzerland, and currently living in Brooklyn, New York, Kimou Meyer (a.k.a. Grotesk) is a graphic artist who is inspired by the global flavors and unbridled energy that pervade New York City's gritty streets. At thirty-something years young, Meyer takes an organic approach to his work and describes his creations as "strange, fanciful, unexpected, and indefinable." Focused on delivering a strong message through the use of vibrant color and simple illustration and type composition, Meyer crafts playful visual narratives that are complex yet easily digestible. He is passionate about folk art, 1950s cartoons, hand-painted signs, old school hip-hop, classic sports, cooking, and his growing family. Over the years, he has executed freelance work for a range of top brands, including Alife, Sixpack France, IRAKNY, 2K by Gingham, UNIQLO, and Fifty24SF. His work has been exhibited in various galleries in Paris, Tokyo, San Francisco, Melbourne, and New York.

GARRETT MORIN

www.garrettmorin.com

Garrett Morin was born in 1980 in Massachusetts and began drawing soon after. In 2004 he graduated from the Rhode Island School of Design and, after working briefly in Los Angeles, moved to Brooklyn, New York, where he currently resides. Morin does freelance art and design for Rad Mountain. His work has appeared in publications such as *Flaunt*, *Complex*, *The Drama*, and *SWINDLE* magazine. Past clients include MTV, Cingular, and Red Bull. He started to experiment with pattern when creating a character called Eloie.

opposite:
Eloie, 2007
Personal project
Pencil on paper

top:
Eloie, 2007
Personal project
Pencil on paper

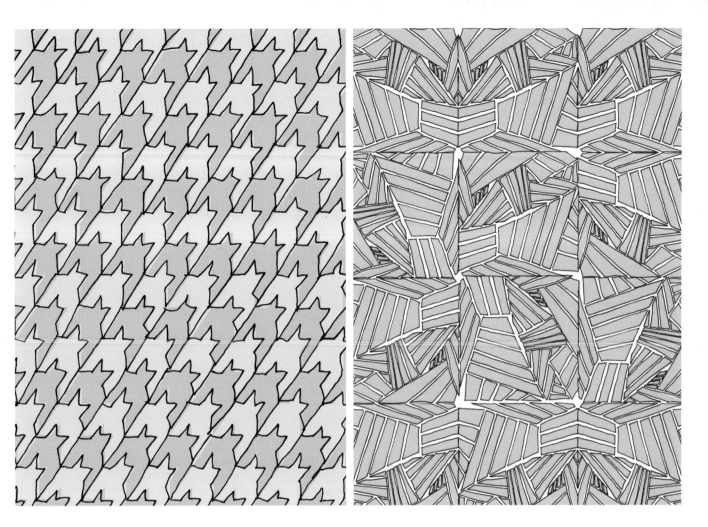

SCOTT NEWLIN

www.scottnewlin.com

Scott Newlin is an industrial designer currently living and working in New York City. He received degrees in both fine arts and industrial design at the California College of the Arts and the University of San Francisco. He has worked with IDEO, Peter Stathis, and Karim Rashid, among others. Newlin's patterns merge simple line art, used to create classic patterns, and the complex gestures of hand-drawn illustration. The effect of the hand, with its subtle motions and striations, creates a depth that is lost when done digitally. He is currently applying his patterns to create limited-edition scarves.

opposite:
Cubes, 2007
Personal project
Pen, ink, and cut paper

top left:
Hand Houndstooth, 2007
Personal project
Pen, ink, and cut paper

top right:
Diagonal Tiles, 2007
Personal project
Pen and ink

MAXWELL PATERNOSTER

www.maxwellp.co.uk

Maxwell Paternoster studied art at Suffolk New College in Ipswich, England, on Saturdays during high school. He continued to attend classes there after graduating high school and eventually completed a full-time national diploma art course. He was then accepted to the illustration degree course at the University of Westminster, London, where he received a three-year degree. During this time he became involved in animation, murals, painting, and video, and illustrated the university magazine. Since leaving school, Paternoster has worked on a range of projects for various clients, including Super Superfical, *Seed* magazine, and Islands Fold. Self-initiated projects play a large role in his work. These have ranged from T-shirt and footwear design to motorcycle customization.

opposite:
3D, 2007
Personal project
Ink on paper

top left:
Technoir, 2007
Personal project
Black ink on paper

top right:
Smokey, 2007
Super Superficial, Soho
Black ink on paper

174–75:
Cashio, 2007
Island Folds
Black ink on paper

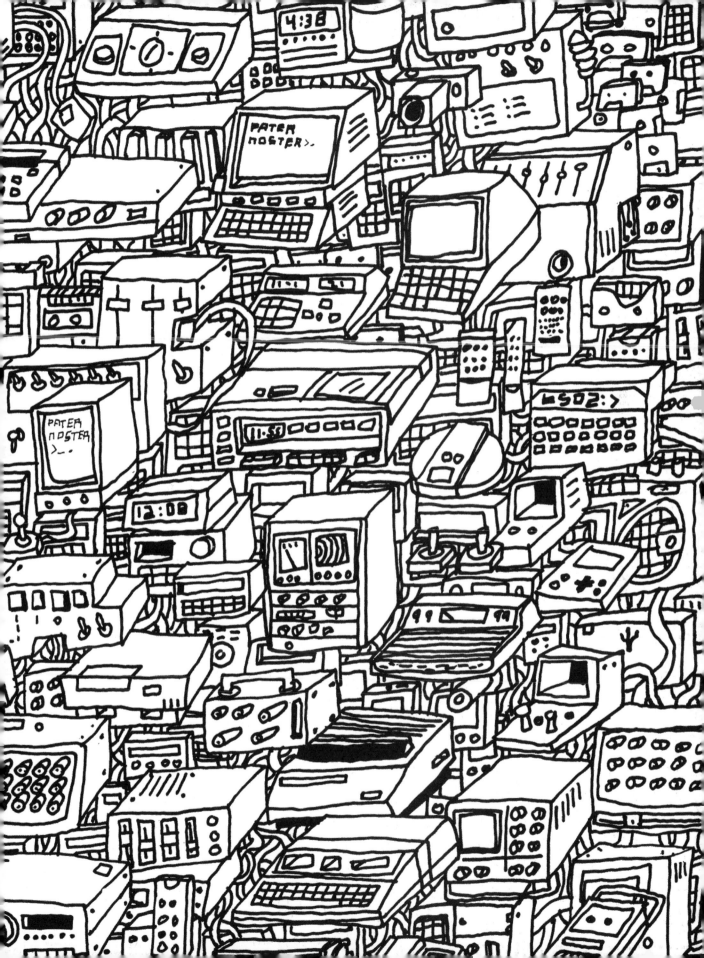

MICHAEL PERRY

www.midwestisbest.com

Michael Perry made this book. He had some very long conversations with himself about whether or not he should be featured. Obviously, he has chosen to be in. When not talking to himself, he runs a small design studio in Brooklyn, New York, working with clients such as Zune, Zoo York, *Dwell* magazine, Chronicle Books, and many more. Perry's first book with Princeton Architectural Press, *Hand Job: A Catalog of Type*, was released in 2007. He also recently started a magazine called *Untitled*, which explores his current interests. Doodling away night and day, Perry creates new typefaces and sundry graphics that inevitably evolve into his new work, exercising his belief that generating piles is the sincerest form of creativity. He has shown his work around the world, from the booming metropolis of London to Los Angeles to the homegrown expanses of Kansas.

opposite:
Untitled Pattern, 2007
Personal project
Watercolor, colored pencil

top left:
Bloob Face, 2007
Ubiquity Records
Pen and computer

top right:
Time & Space, 2008
6 Pack
Marker

178:
Exploding Shapes, 2007
2x4 Shirts
Pen and computer

179:
All Together Now, 2007
Personal Project
Pen and computer

180–81:
Optical 004, 2006
Arkitip magazine
Pen and computer

PIETARI POSTI

www.pposti.com

Pietari Posti was born in Helsinki, Finland, in the late 1970s. When other kids asked him to play, he preferred to stay in and draw. Later they stopped asking. Nowadays he spends his days and nights illustrating both in the traditional way and by computer, and, more often, using both. Since 2005 Posti has been working as a freelance illustrator in Barcelona. His works have been featured in American Airlines' *American Way* magazine, *Dazed & Confused* magazine, *Time Out London*, and Volvo.

opposite:
Giants, Birdy, 2007
Personal project
Mixed media

top left:
Swan, 2007
Hansa Print
Mixed media

top right:
Giants, Deer, 2007
Personal project
Mixed media

LUKE RAMSEY

www.islandsfold.com

Luke Ramsey's primary creative focus is on Islands Fold, a free artist residency created with his partner, Angela Conley. They make art books and zines to fund their project and have collaborated with over forty artists. Ramsey's creative language has been heavily influenced by the d.i.y. punk movement, Prem Rawat's message of peace, and artists ranging from Keith Haring to Keith Jones. Ramsey explores the possibility of art, which doesn't always conform to gallery walls. Although once in a while he'll hang a frame or two, he prefers mailing zines to people.

opposite:
Sex Head Hill, 2006
Personal project
Pen

top left:
Wise Beard, 2006
Personal project
Pen

top right:
Neo Doodles, 2004
Personal project
Pen

186–87:
In Arm's Length, 2006
Islands Fold, by Peter Taylor
and Luke Ramsey
Pen

188–89:
Octoluva, 2006
Personal project
Pen

190–91:
Galactic Milkshake, 2006
Islands Fold, by Daniel Gonzalez
and Luke Ramsey
Pen

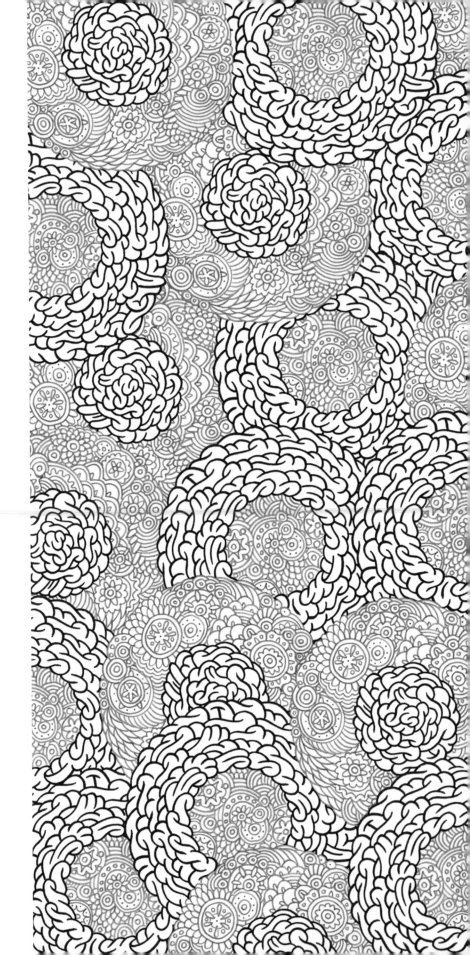

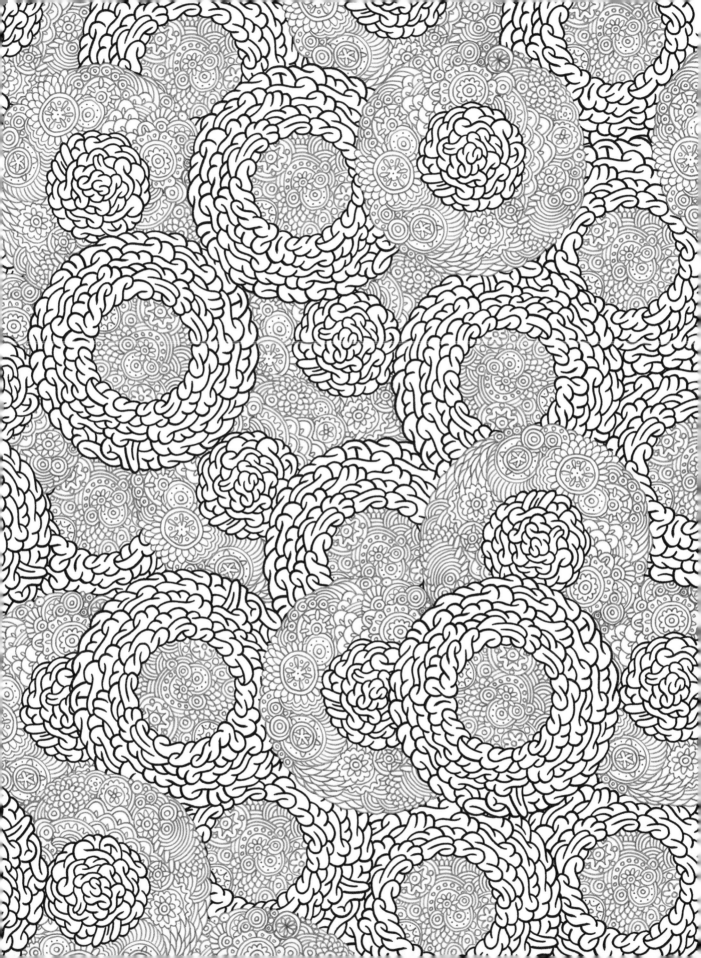

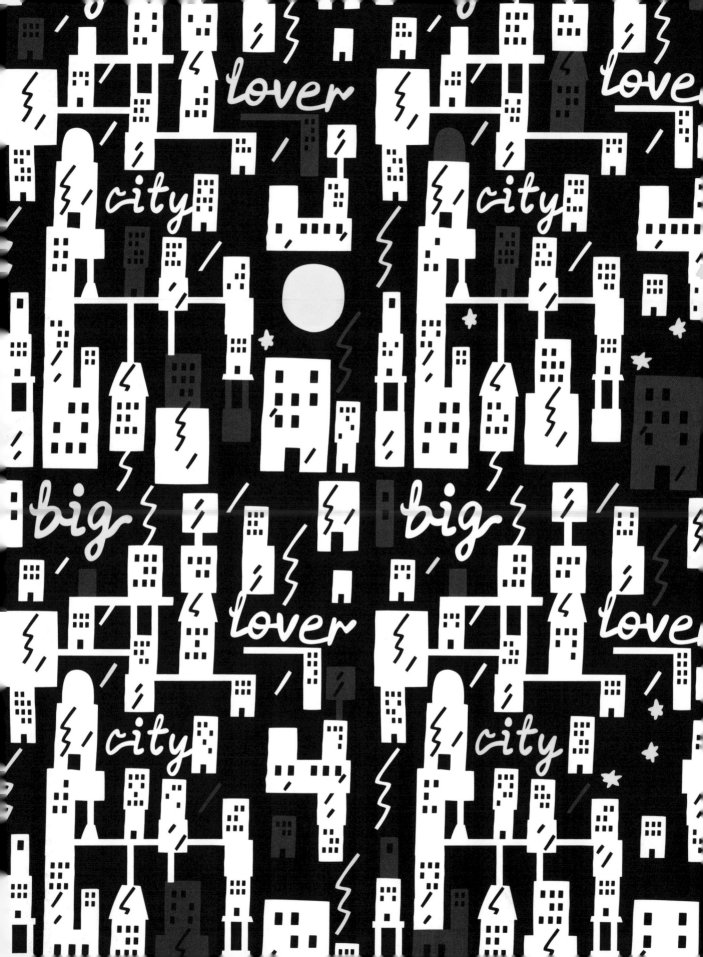

ANDREAS SAMUELSSON

www.andreassamuelsson.com

A freelance illustrator based in Stockholm, Sweden, Andreas Samuelsson works for clients such as Human Empire, the *Walrus*, and *Odd Magazine*. He draws inspiration from memories of music, movies, TV shows, video games and stuff from childhood, people he has met or seen, strange situations, dreams, and deep thoughts.

opposite:
Big City Lover, 2006
Personal project
Pen and computer

top left:
Kit 01, 2006
Personal project
Pen and computer

top right:
Choose Shoes, 2007
Personal project
Pen and computer

194–95:
Back to School, 2007
Personal project
Pen and computer

196–97:
Hagabion's Café, 2007
Hagabion's Café
Pen and computer

199–201
The Quiet Revolution, 2006–07
Personal project
Drawn black-and-white lines

CLAIRE SCULLY

www.thequietrevolution.co.uk

Claire Scully received her BA in graphic and media design from London College of Communication in 2004 and her MA in communication design from London's Central Saint Martins College of Art and Design in 2006. As well as continually working on personal projects and frequently collaborating with various artists, Scully works as a freelance illustrator. The Quiet Revolution is a body of work that combines printed illustrations with moving images inspired by the conflicting and harmonious relationships the urban environment has with the natural world. Scully attempts to subvert the familiar and overlooked into a sinister surreal situation using mutation and juxtapositions.

YUKO SHIMIZU

www.yukoart.com

Yuko Shimizu is an illustrator, educator, and not-so-prolific-at-this-moment fine artist. After receiving a BA in advertising and marketing from Waseda University, Tokyo, she got a position in public relations in corporate Tokyo. It was a decent job that never made her happy and she had a midlife crisis at the age of twenty-two. It still took her more than ten years to figure out what she really wanted to do and to save just enough money so she could go back to school full-time for four more years. That is how she came back to New York City, where she spent her childhood, and enrolled in the School of Visual Arts (SVA). Shimizu received her MFA in the Illustration as Visual Essay program in 2003 and has been illustrating freelance since, producing work for clients such as Microsoft, T-Mobile, MTV, *The New Yorker*, and the *New York Times*. She also teaches in the illustration department at SVA. She works in SHY Studio in midtown Manhattan, a space that she shares with two wonderful artist friends whom she considers her New York family. Art is a never-ending learning process which often times can be painful, but Shimizu loves everything about it, and has not had a midlife crisis since.

opposite:
Frog Calendar, 2007
Dellas Graphics
Pen and computer

top left:
Swimmers, 2006
The *Walrus*
Pen and computer

top right:
Storage, 2005
Storage magazine
Pen and computer

204–205:
DJ Slip, 2005
Plus et Plus
Pen and computer

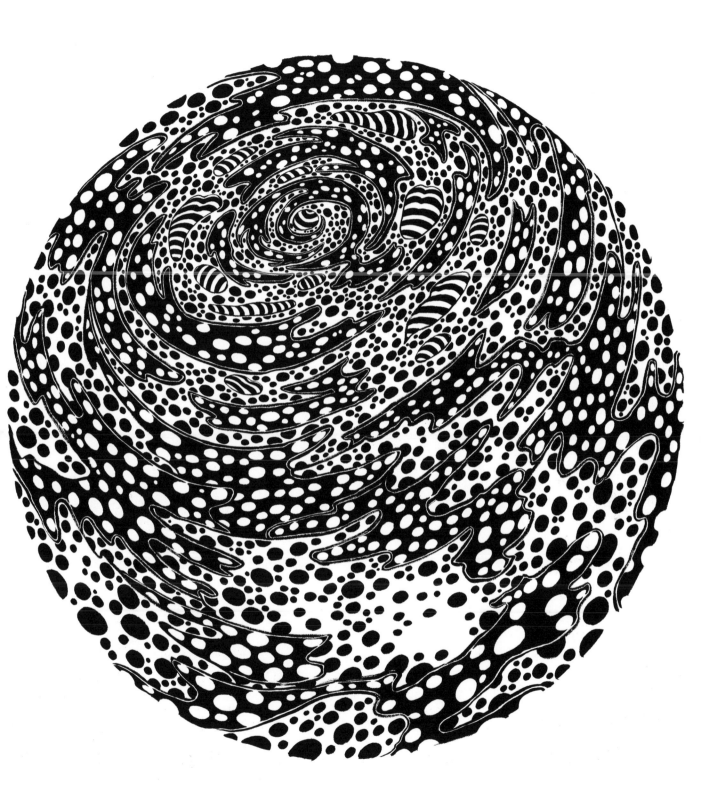

MAJA STEN

www.majasten.se

Maja Sten lives and works in Stockholm, Sweden. Since graduating from the Royal College of Art in London in 2002, she has worked as a freelance illustrator in a wide range of fields, such as editorial, product design, advertising, books, self-initiated projects, and exhibitions. She is also a guest tutor and lecturer at Stockholm's Konstfack, University College of Arts, Crafts, and Design, where she once was a student herself.

opposite:
Jazzy, 2006
Personal project
Markers

top left:
Big Dots, 2006
Personal project
Markers

top right:
Paradise, 2006
Personal project
Pen and computer

208–9:
Scheherazade Remix, 2003
Personal project
Silkscreen posters

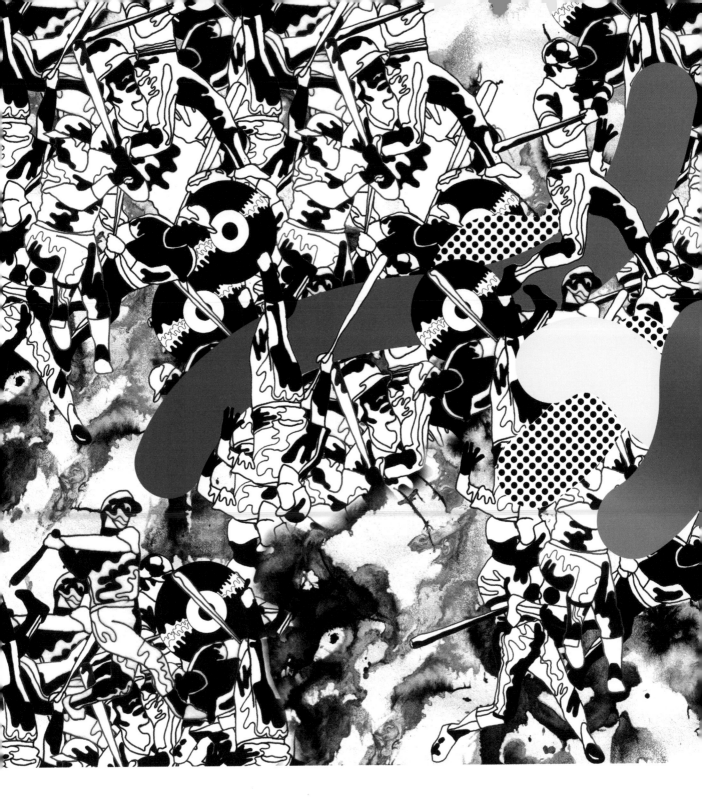

TRAVIS STEARNS

www.iammintcondition.com

Travis Stearns was born in the north woods of Minnesota in 1983. His favorite shape is the circle. He likes sleeping, discovering music, tattoos, Pontiac Firebirds, the color black, calculators, mountain men, agates, wild rice soup, hippies, Italo disco, and airbrushed T-shirts. Someday, he would like to move way up north, deep into the forest, to build a studio surrounded by nothing. For now, he works on projects for a variety of clients such as IAMSOUND Records, the Moon Goons, *SWINDLE* magazine, and his friend Jonathan Ackerman.

opposite:
Heavyhittaz EP, 2006
Curtis Vodka / Flamin' Hotz
Pen

211–13:
Patterns 1–4, 2006
Personal project
Pen

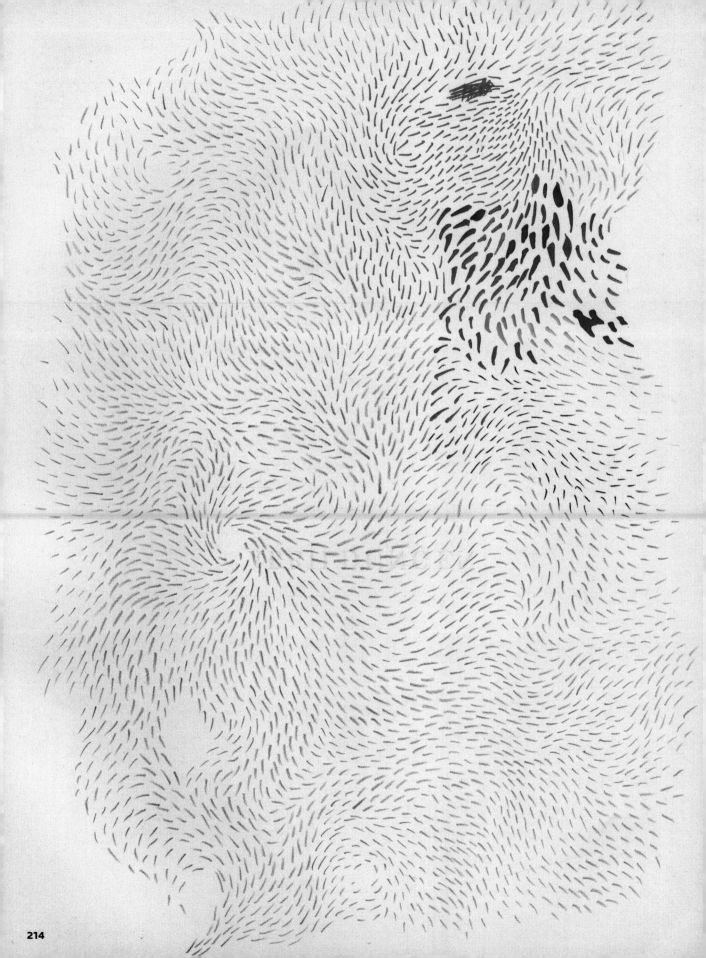

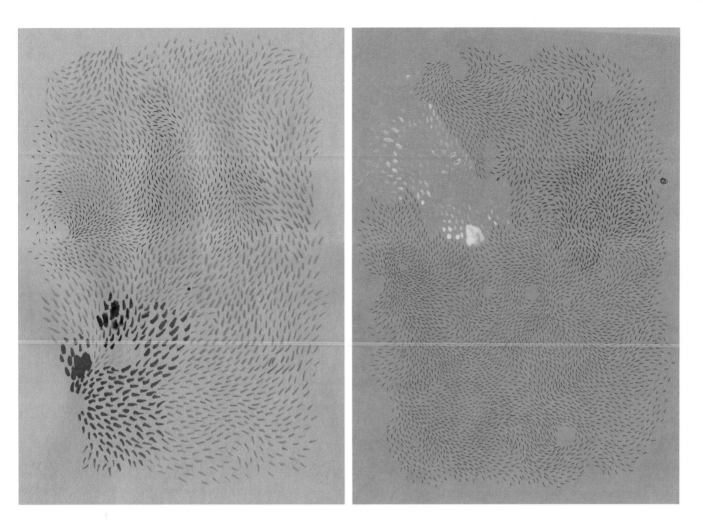

HOLLY STEVENSON

www.hollystevenson.com

Holly Stevenson is an artist living and working in New York City. She earned her BA from Pratt Institute School of Art and Design and currently teaches design at Parsons The New School for Design. She creates artwork for gallery exhibitions as well as for commercial clients. She likes experimenting with patterns.

opposite:
Long Truth, 2007
Personal project
Pencil, pen, and paint on found paper

top left:
Hot and Fun, 2007
Personal project
Pencil, pen, and paint on bleached
construction paper

top right:
Bad Beak, 2007
Personal project
Pencil, pen, and paint on bleached
construction paper

216–17:
Monarch Bush, 2007
Personal project
Pencil and pen on found paper

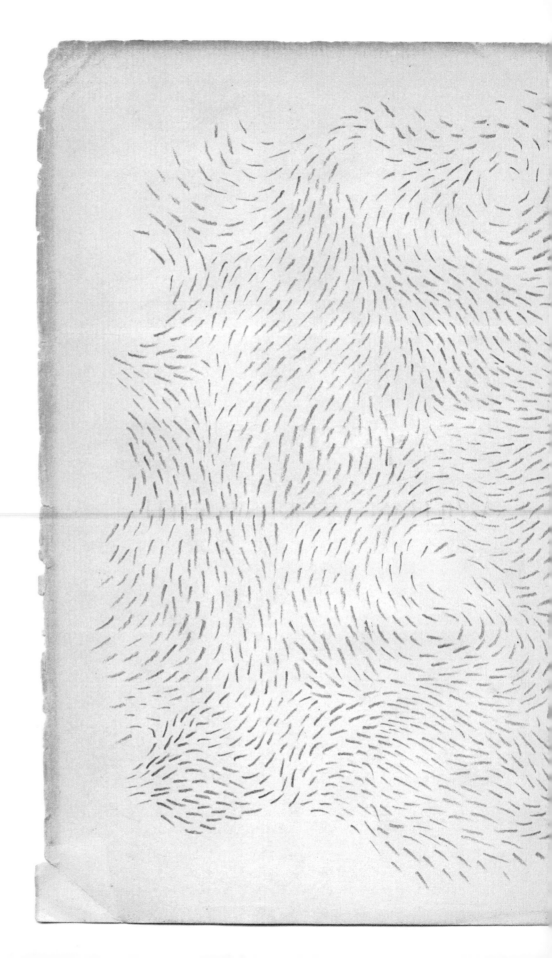

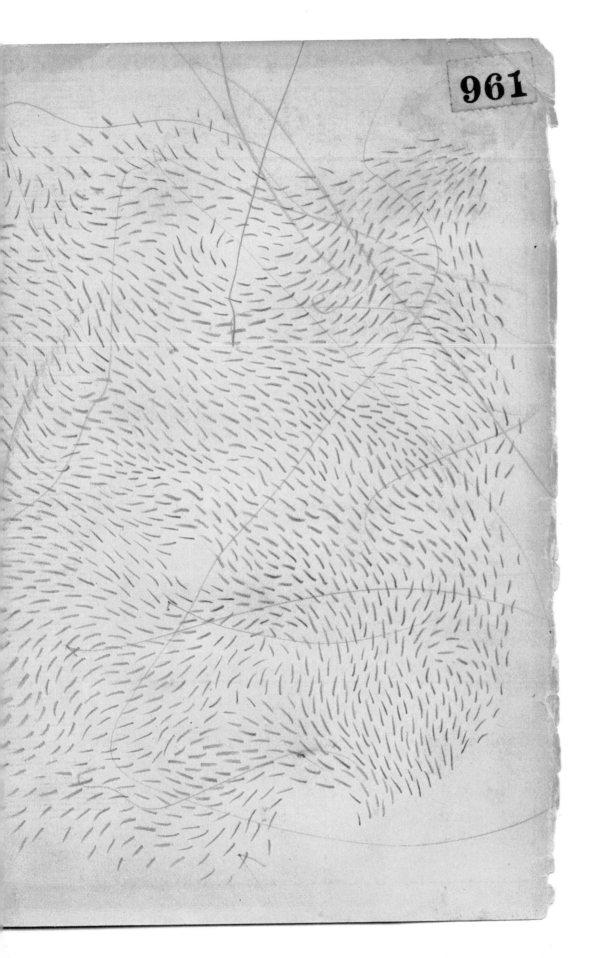

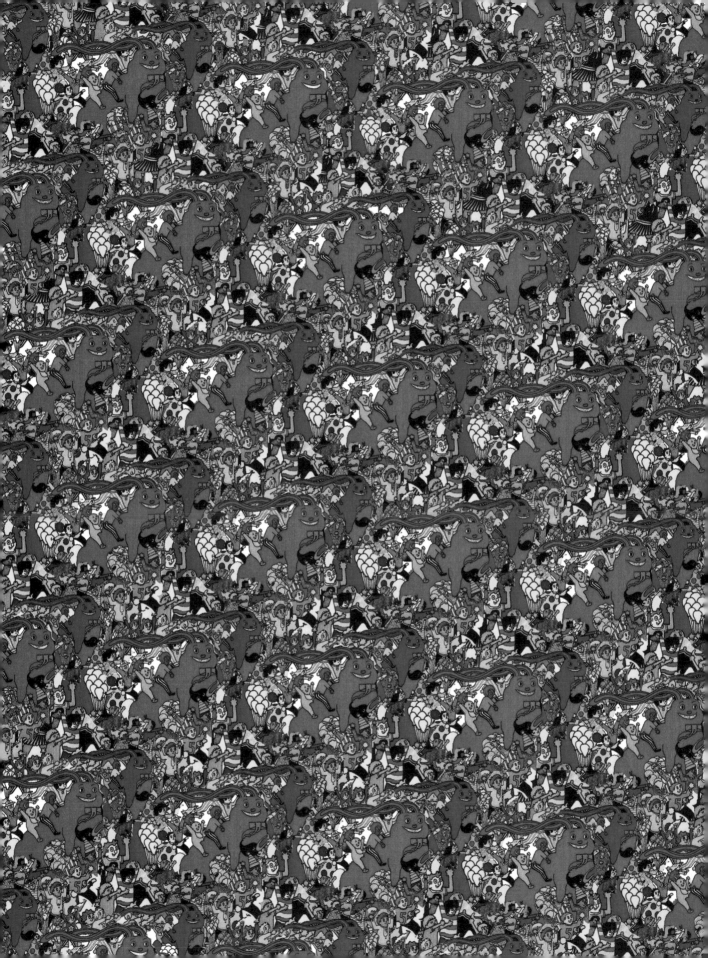

JIM STOTEN

www.jimtheillustrator.co.uk

Jim the Illustrator, a.k.a. Jim Stoten, studied at the University of Brighton, England, for three years and then moved to London, where he joined Heart Agency in October 2005. Recently, Jim completed his first graphic novel, *The Diamond*, and is now looking for a publisher. His work has been featured in *Amelia's Magazine*, *Dazed & Confused*, *Cream*, *Beat*, and *Gomez*.

opposite:
Rabbit Parade, 2007
Personal project
Pen, paper, and computer

top left:
The Attack of the Modern Server, 2006
CIO magazine
Pen and paper

top right:
Vision of the Future Year 2007, 2006
The *Guardian*
Pen and paper

220:
My Mind Wallpaper, 2007
Personal project
Pen, paper, and computer

221:
Jabba Gets Ready for the Party, 2007
Cream magazine
Pen and paper

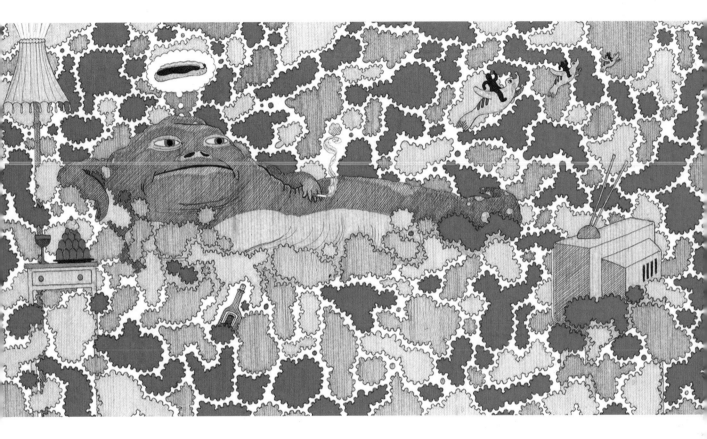

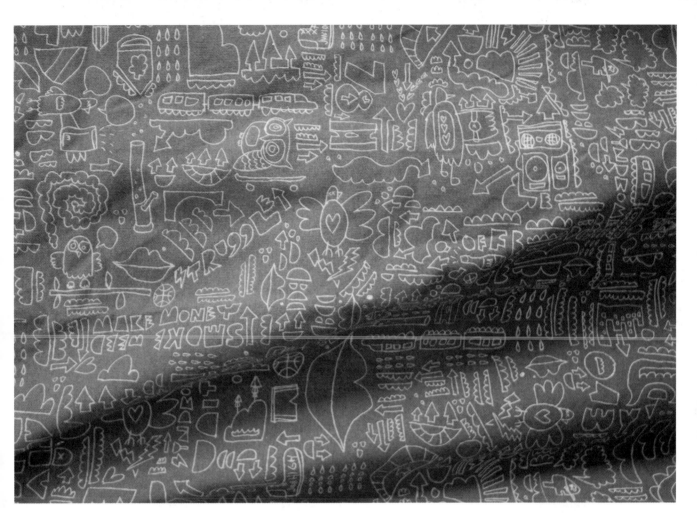

STRUGGLE INC.

www.struggleinc.com

Cody Hudson, who works under the name Struggle Inc., is a Chicago-based commercial artist and painter. He is known for work that has a bold, organic, and modern feel to it. He has worked on everything from skateboard graphics to national billboard campaigns to mix tape covers. His paintings have been exhibited throughout the United States, Europe, and Japan. He enjoys ice fishing, drinking Old Style beer, and things made of wood.

BETSY WALTON

www.morningcraft.com

After spending a few years in a few cubicles, Betsy Walton made a break for it. She works full time as an artist and illustrator from her studio in Portland, Oregon. Her recent work explores the possibilities of visual narrative. With a background primarily in printmaking and drawing, Betsy experiments with layering, detail, and color in her works on paper. When she is not painting and drawing, Betsy might be found wandering through the library, or exploring the forests and beaches of Oregon.

opposite:
Two Teas, 2006
Personal project
Gouache painting on paper

top left:
White Crackle, 2006
Personal project
Gouache painting on paper

top right:
Seeing Eyes, 2006
Personal project
Gouache painting on paper

230:
Exploding Egg Rainbow Quilt Mountain,
2007
Personal project
Gouache and pencil painting on paper

231:
Making It Happen, 2007
Personal project
Gouache and pencil painting on paper

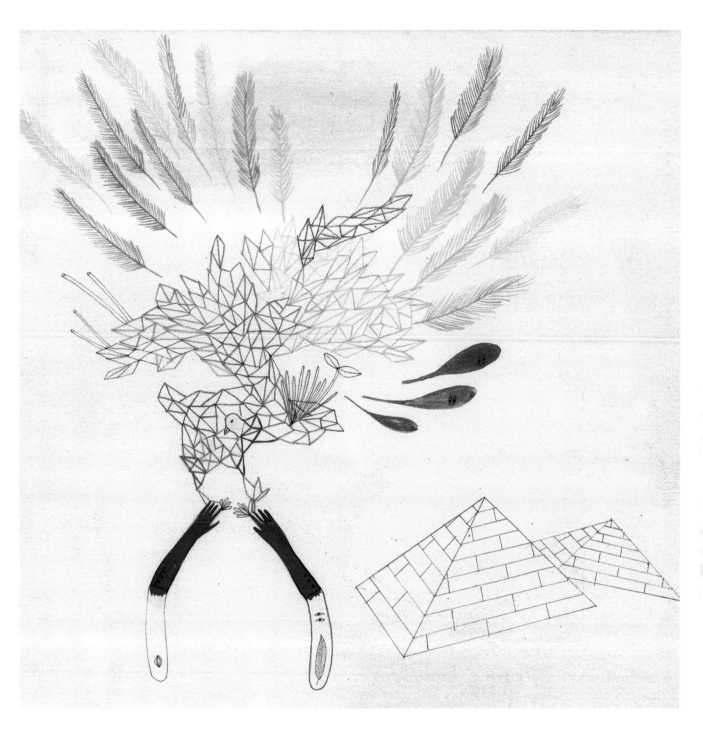

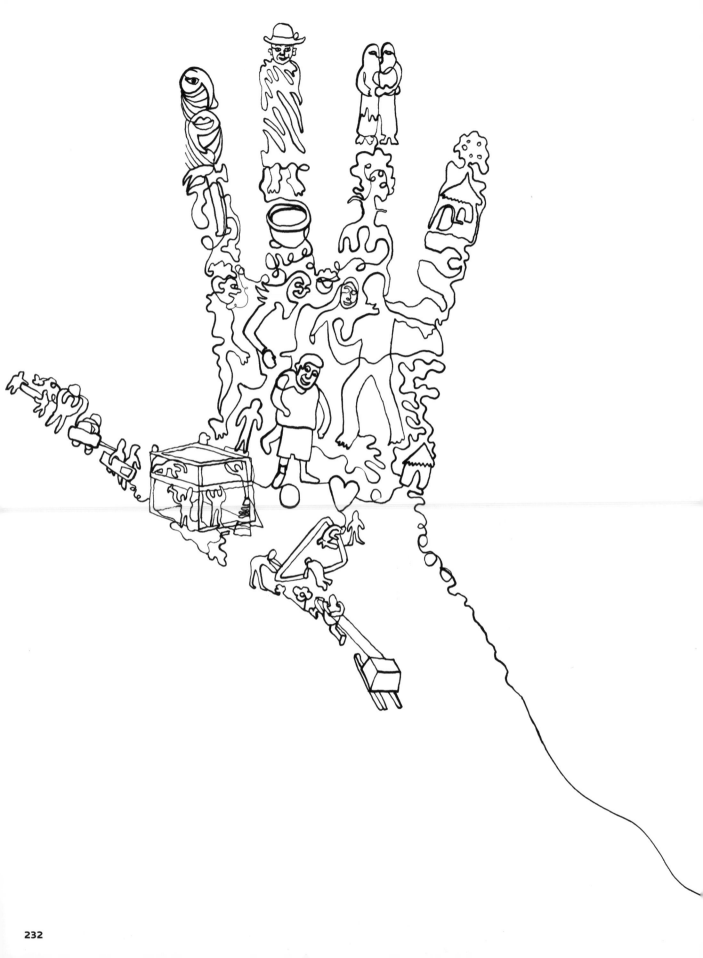

BEN WEEKS

www.benweeks.ca

Ben Weeks has been running his Toronto-based studio for three years since finishing his MA at the University of Huddersfield, England, and leaving brand consultancy firm ATTIK. His work has since won awards from D&AD, *STEP inside design*, *Black Book*, *Graphis*, *American Illustration*, *Applied Arts*, *Coupe*, and the Association of Illustrators. He enjoys telling stories with pictures and typography.

opposite:
Concert Crowd Concept, 2007
Youthography/Riot
Mixed media

top:
Honda Fit Campaign, 2006
Honda/Grip Limited
Pen

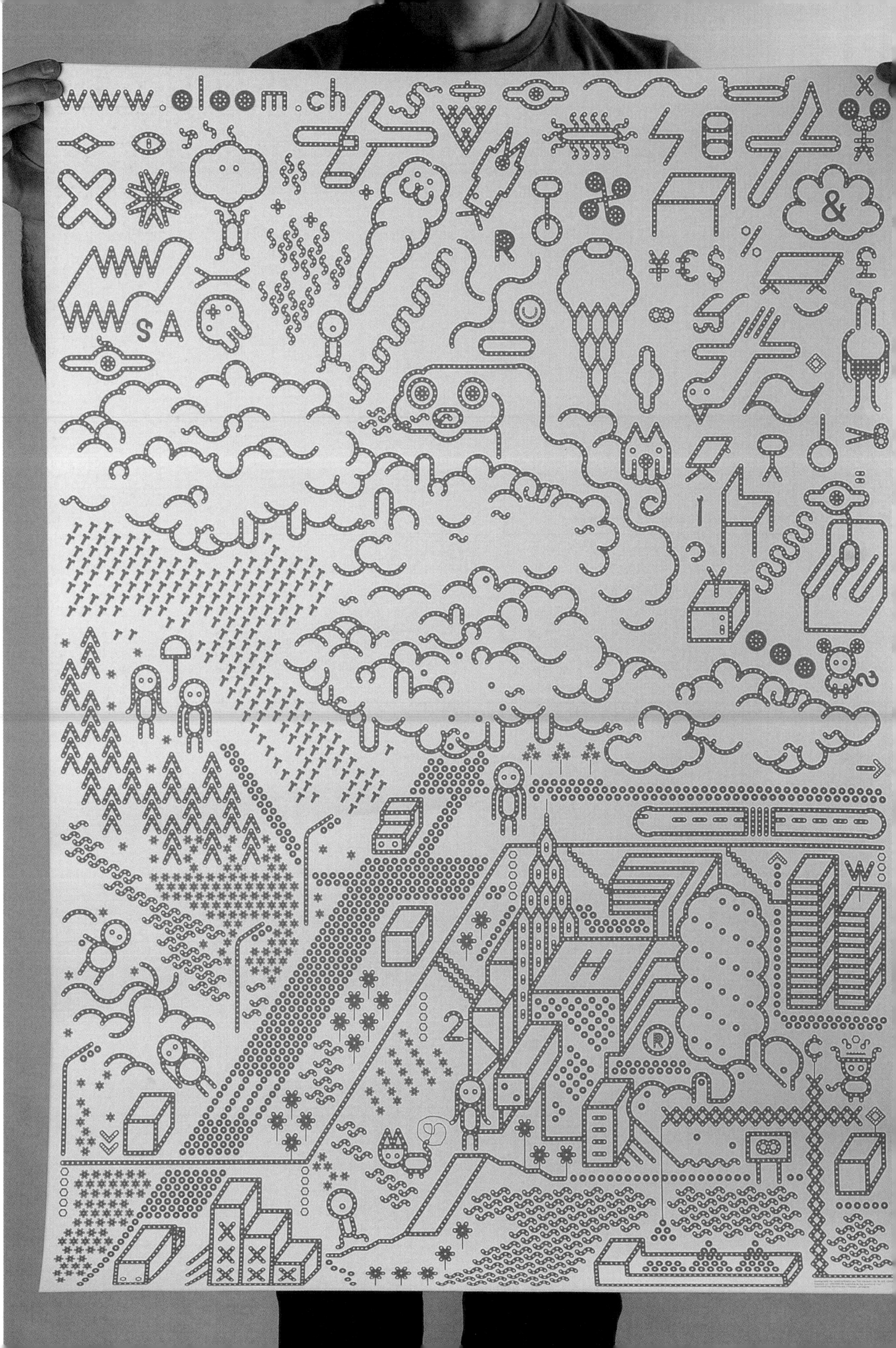
www.oloom.ch

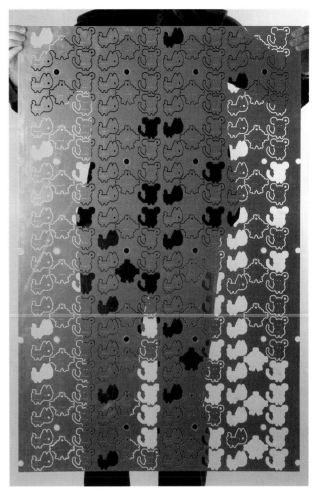

234–37:
Oloom Visual Identity, 2006
Oloom
Pen and computer

WELCOMETO

www.welcometo.as

Adam Macháček and Sébastien Bohner, one Czech and one Swiss, met while working as interns at Studio Dumbar in Rotterdam, the Netherlands. Two foreigners, they traveled around the country together. When their internship was about to end, as a present for their colleagues, they made Flash animations based on their Dutch observations. That was the first work they made together, and since then they have collaborated on a number of projects for Chronicle Books, *Computer Arts* magazine, and the Moravian Gallery in the Czech Republic.

Théâtre de Vevey · 4 rue du Théâtre · 1800 Vevey · tél021 925 94 94

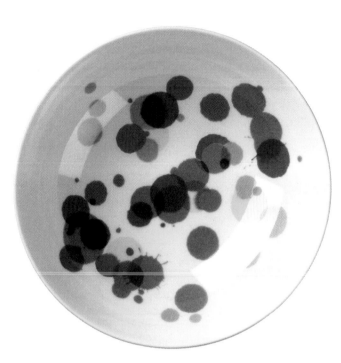

HANNA WERNING

www.byhanna.com

Hanna Werning studied graphic design at Central Saint Martins College of Art and Design in London, where she also worked for six years in various fields such as advertising, television, multimedia, and art. A Swedish citizen, she returned to her mother country in the summer of 2004 and founded her own studio in Stockholm. Werning has been most recognized for her *AnimalFlowers wallpaper-posters*, which can be used both as a single poster and as wallpaper. She has also designed prints for Boråstapeter, Borås Cotton, IKEA, Rörstrand, Eastpak, and the fashion label Dagmar, and has lectured and held workshops at various design colleges as well as at the Nationalmuseum in Stockholm, Sweden.

opposite:
AnimalFlowers, 2001–04
Personal project
Wallpaper

top left:
ID Rörstrand (bowl), 2007
Rörstrand
Porcelain decor

top right:
Cherry Sheep Bittersweet, 2007
Lagom
Wrapping paper

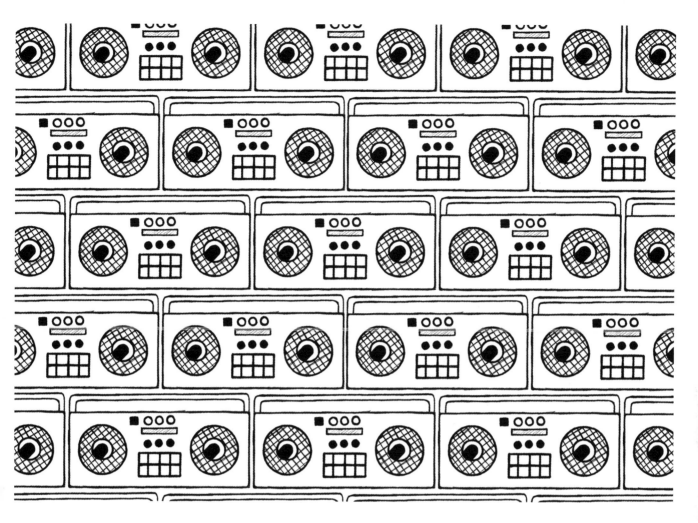

MAYA WILD

<u>www.mayawild.com</u>

Maya Wild is an illustrator and art director based in London. She regularly contributes to many magazines worldwide, including *Dazed & Confused* and *Nylon*. She has recently worked on projects for Britain's Channel 4 and Urban Outfitters. She also designs fabric patterns and album cover artwork and has exhibited her drawings at galleries in Paris, London, and Tokyo. In addition to her solo work, she is one half of the drawing, animation, and set design team The Boos, who are currently working on animations for a documentary feature film.

opposite:
Untitled, 2007
Personal project
Drawn patterns for use on
T-shirts and fabric

top:
Untitled, 2007
Personal project
Drawn patterns for use on
T-shirts and fabric

242:
Untitled, 2007
Personal project
Drawn patterns for use on
T-shirts and fabric

242:
Untitled, 2007
Personal project
Drawn patterns for use on
T-shirts and fabric

244:
Untitled, 2007
Personal project
Drawn patterns for use on
T-shirts and fabric

245:
Untitled, 2007
Personal project
Drawn patterns for use on
T-shirts and fabric

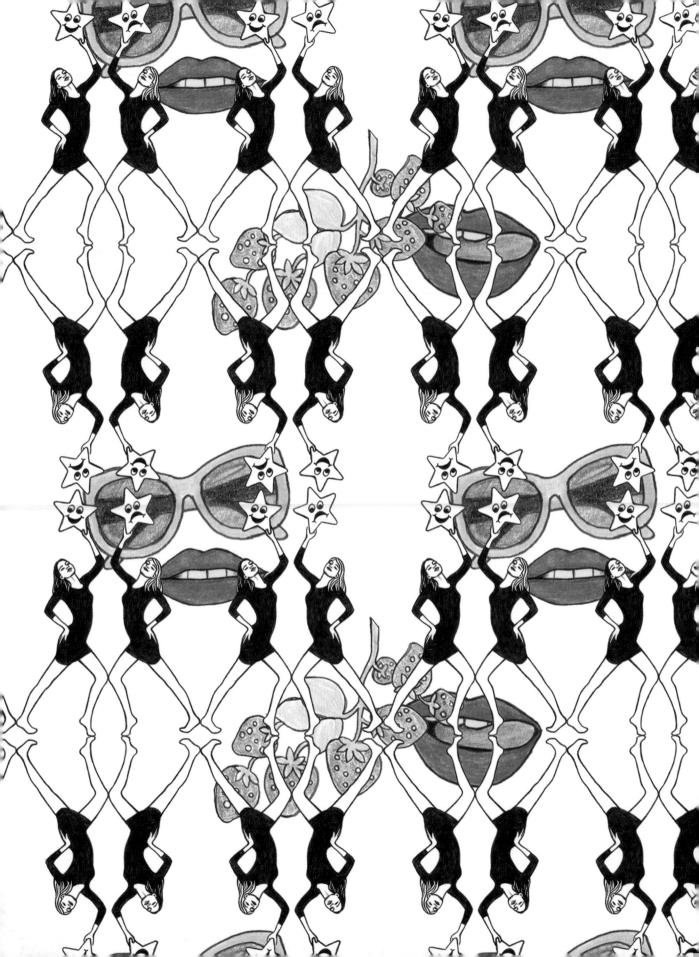

YOKOLAND

www.yokoland.com

246–51:
Parergon: Journal for
Contemporary Music, 2006–07
Parergon
Four-color offset print

Yokoland is a graphic design and illustration studio that was started by Espen Friberg and Aslak Gurholt Rønsen sometime between their graduation from high school (2000) and their graduation from the Oslo National Academy of the Arts, Norway (2004/2005). In the beginning, there was no intention for Yokoland to be a graphic design studio (it sort of happened along the way). Yokoland was just a place to experiment with various small projects. Today, designer Thomas Tengesdal Nordby is also part of Yokoland.

Yokoland mainly focuses on print-based projects like books, magazines, posters, and album covers. The studio also works across various media, creating signage, set design, wall paintings, exhibition design, short films, music videos, title sequences, and websites, and also does more commercial work like company identities and advertising. From time to time Yokoland has their own exhibitions and participates in group exhibitions.

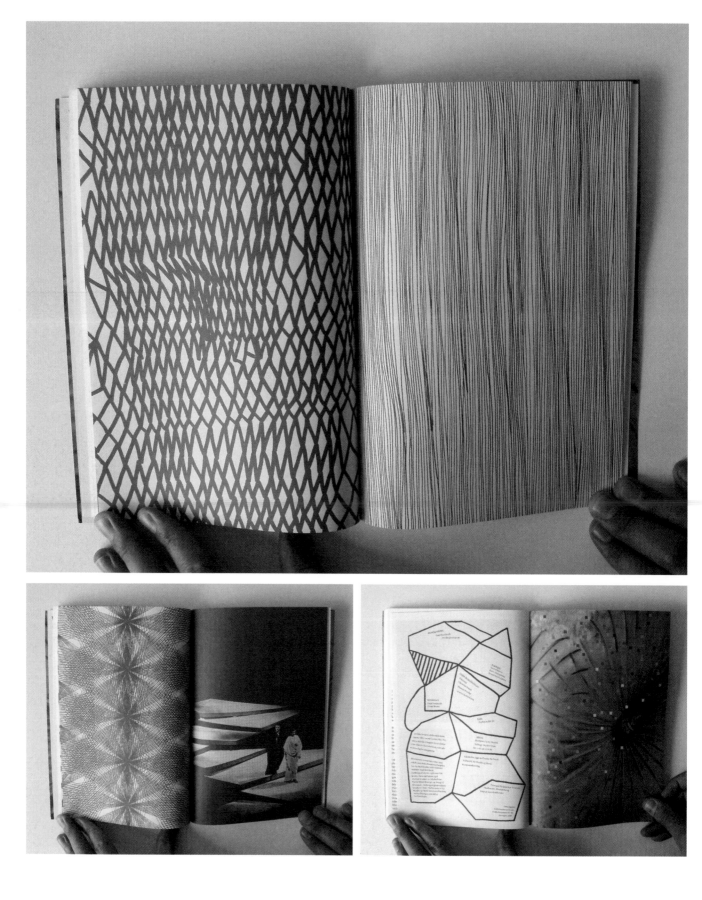

Festivalomtaler

Om å oppfordre til lytting

Noen betraktninger om Ultima-konserten med Ensemble Court-circuit og dirigent Pierre-André Valade i Kulturkirken Jakob 05.10.06

Av: Gjertrud Pedersen

Vignett

I leksikon leser jeg at en kortslutning oppstår når to punkter i et elektrisk anlegg forbindes gjennom en svært lav ledningsmotstand. Kortslutningen vil føre til en lysbue, og denne lysbuen vil brenne helt til strømmen brytes. Det kan være mange årsaker til en kortslutning, for eksempel slett håndverk, dårlig isolerte ledninger – eller en altfor stor fugl som havner litt forkjært i et elektrisk anlegg. Hvor stor må fuglen være for å sette i gang en kortslutning? Er det tilstrekkelig å være en slags trost? Eller er det nødvendig med en mye større fugl, kanskje en struts? Er det relevant hvorvidt fuglen kan fly?

Musikk kan berøre oss sterkt og en musikalsk opplevelse kan åpne en ny verden for oss. Det å være bevisst hvordan man presenterer musikken på en konsert, krever at man tar valg, og det å ta valg kan ofte være risikabelt. Imidlertid tror jeg at man gjennom å ta valg i en formidlingssituasjon kan bidra til å åpne noe som for publikum kan være en inngang til musikken. Det handler om å oppfordre til lytting. Jeg savnet en slik oppfordring på denne konserten.

Uhørte harmonier, visuell støy og en usedvanlig rik klangverden

Konserten åpnet med *L'Harmonie des Sphères* av den franske komponisten Allain Gaussin. For Pythagoras var sfærenes musikk noe som ble skapt under planetenes omdreininger, og for ham hadde hvert himmellegeme sin egen lyd. I utgangspunktet var ikke denne musikken hørbar for det menneskelige øre, men det var mulig å lære seg dette.

Gaussins harmonier framsto som et gåtefullt spill mellom gjentagelser, klangflater, transformasjoner og brudd. De ørsmå musikerne oppstod under konstellasjoner, noe som åpnet for mange ulike klanger. Lydbildet var meget nyansert i de minste

besetningene, og særlig gjorde et parti med fiolin, cello og slagverk stort inntrykk. Her spiller slagverkeren med køller på Brygelets strenger, og dette skapte klanger som jeg ikke klarer å beskrive på noen annen måte enn at det var utrolig vakkert.

Et navn kan gi mange assosiasjoner, og jeg tror det kan være et viktig element i lytteropplevelsen å kjenne tittelen til et musikkverk. I Ultimafestivalens programbok og i det A4-arket med programinformasjon som ble delt ut på konserten, sto Gaussins verk kun oppført med tittelen Nytt verk. Det er selvsagt mulig at tittelen på verket har kommet til svært sent i prosessen, men jeg syns det er underlig at man ikke hadde tatt seg bryet med å trykke tittelen *L'Harmonie des Sphères* kan åpne opp for nye tankebaner og berike lytteropplevelsen, og jeg skulle ønske jeg hadde fått vite tittelen da jeg var på konserten. Istedenfor å finne ut dette i ettertid.

Rolf Wallin har hentet tittelen *The Age of Wire and String* fra debutromanen til den amerikanske forfatteren Ben Marcus (f. 1967; romanen kom ut i 1996). Wallins komposisjon består av åtte musikalske miniatyrer, og disse bærer også titler fra Marcus' roman. Titlene er både oppsiktsvekkende og tankevekkende, som for eksempel *Sneering*, *Mechanical Speech* og *Leg of Brother who Died Early*, og jeg syns det er underlig at heller ikke disse titlene er kommet på arket med programinformasjon. Minimyrbetegnelsene står riktignok i Ultimas programbok men det er verkomtalene ordnet alfabetisk, og det er dermed ingen ting som knytter *The Age of Wire and String* til de andre verkene på denne konserten. Slik blir konserten en presentasjon av fire enkeltstående verk, uten at disse relateres til hverandre på noen annen måte enn at vi får høre dem over hverandre i tid.

Å høre hver og en av de åtte miniatyrene i Wallins *The Age of Wire and String* var som å være med på en oppdagelsesreise. Hver miniatyr var som var lyst og lett, noe var flyktig som et pust, noe var preget av horisontale linjer, noe annet var hastig og perkusivt, noe var lyrisk og noe annet var utholdt. Wallins musikk er ubyre kontant, og det gir hver eneste tone stor verdi. Hver miniatyr blir klippet brått av, noe som slik ring til å vedre om kanskje hver miniatyr var et fragment av noe større. Eller, for å spisse videre på Gaussins tittel, kanskje det er mulig å tenke seg at musikken slik stupper, turn at det fortsatte i en annen sfære der den ikke lenger var hørbar? Etter den brutale minimyrene måtte jeg med sorg innse at turen var over, og jeg kan bare håpe at jeg snart får anledning til å høre dette musikkverket igjen.

Etter pause fikk vi høre Ashwin Schaathuns verk *Ragalen (+62+)* for ni instrumenter. Av

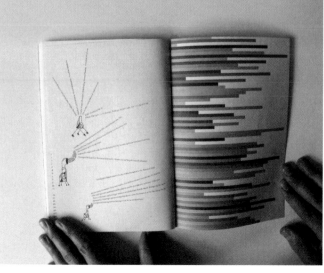

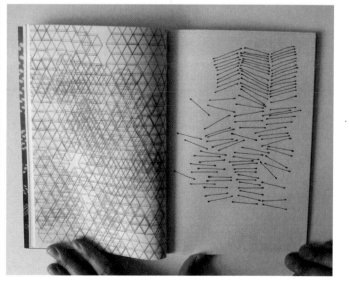

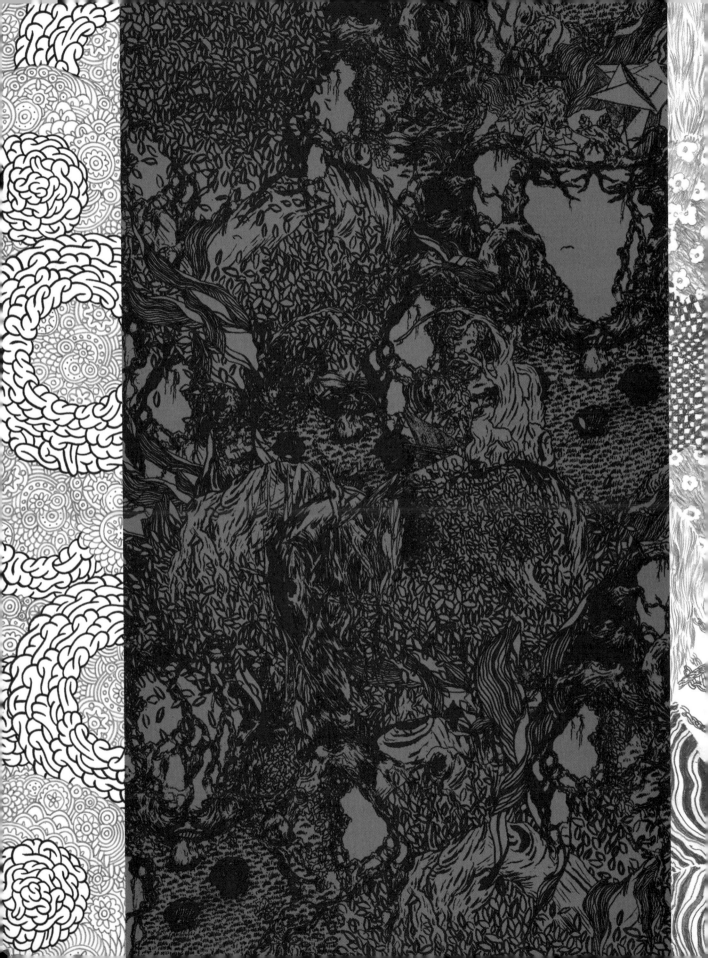

IMAGES BY LUKE RAMSEY AND ANNA GIERTZ